My Southern-Fried Search for the Meaning of Life

Sam McLeod

A TOUCHSTONE BOOK
Published by Simon & Schuster

New York   London   Toronto   Sydney

Touchstone
A Division of Simon & Schuster, Inc.
1230 Avenue of the Americas
New York, NY 10020

First Touchstone hardcover edition June 2010

TOUCHSTONE and colophon are registered trademarks of Simon & Schuster, Inc.

For information about special discounts for bulk purchases,
please contact Simon & Schuster Special Sales at 1-866-506-1949
or business@simonandschuster.com.

The Simon & Schuster Speakers Bureau can bring authors to your live event.
For more information or to book an event contact the Simon & Schuster Speakers Bureau
at 1-866-248-3049 or visit our website at www.simonspeakers.com.

Designed by Ruth Lee-Mui

Manufactured in the United States of America

10 9 8 7 6 5 4 3 2 1

Library of Congress Cataloging-in-Publication Data
McLeod, Sam.
   Big appetite : my Southern-fried search for the meaning of life / by Sam McLeod.
      p.   cm.
1. McLeod, Sam—Childhood and youth.   2. McLeod, Sam—Health.
3. Overweight persons—Biography.   4. Food habits—Southern States.
5. Cookery, American—Southern style.   I. Title.
CT275.M4653813A3 2010
394.1'20975—dc22
                                                                    2010011364

ISBN 978-1-4391-8816-3
ISBN 978-1-4391-8881-1 (ebook)

This book is dedicated to the wonderful women who fed me fried chicken, barbecued chicken, fried catfish, chicken and dumplings, meatloaf, country ham biscuits with red-eye gravy, pulled pork on corncakes with coleslaw, steak biscuits, chicken deluxe, chicken spaghetti, pork chop casserole, company shrimp casserole, eggplant Parmesan, Brunswick stew, tuna noodle casserole with potato chips on top, egg with a hole in the middle, beef stew, shrimp and grits, sausage gravy and biscuits, corn pudding, fried okra, fried green tomatoes, boiled potatoes with white sauce, potato salad, tangy marinated vegetables, oyster casserole, macaroni and cheese *and* oysters (yep, that's right), turkey dressing without the turkey, squash casserole, tomato pie, raspberry Jell-O salad (without nuts or celery) served on iceberg lettuce leaves with a dollop of homemade mayonnaise, lime Jell-O salad, ginger ale salad, deviled eggs, pickled shrimp, shrimp dip, tuna salad sandwiches on white bread with the crusts cut off, salmon salad sandwiches with red onion slices and horseradish, pimento cheese sandwiches, toasted cheese and onion sandwiches, sweet onion hushpuppies, cornbread sticks, spoon bread, yeasty dinner rolls, biscuits, strawberry pie, chess pie, bitter lemon bars, oatmeal cookies, boiled custard, apple butter, fig preserves, pickled okra, cranberry apple relish, and Sunday-afternoon sun tea.

A special thank you to my wife, Annie, who disputes much of what I write about her, but usually gets over it; to Coco, my mother, who made this book possible and crawled under the guest-room bed (where it was really dusty) to get the pictures for us; to Jolley people everywhere; to my beautiful daughters, handsome son-in-law, and the rest of the family for their good-looking and good-natured support; to Candace, who helped me with initial edits and the cool map; to Phyllis and Judy, who edited my work and each other's and helped make this book better; to Liv, who patiently led me into this; to Trish and many others at Simon & Schuster who turned manuscript into book and got it to where you could get it; to Uncle Joe, Cousin Joe, Pat, Kelly, and all the good folks at Waffle House for their encouragement, promotional support, and the waffles; to Sarah and Codger John for the unusually good pictures of yours truly; to Boots, who taught me the meaning of A; to my old friend Gordon, who handed me the answer; to Dorothy at the Old Country Store in Jackson, Tennessee, a gracious lady and a great cook who showed me how to make fried green tomatoes and fried cracklin' bread; to Ray, Squire, Deb, Matt, Shirley, Clark, Juanita, Gretchen, Les, Big Frank (he didn't really do anything, but he'll whine like a baby if I leave him out), and the good people of Walla Walla. (Yes, it's a real place.)

AUTHOR'S NOTE

Some of the events in this book happened as described. Some were embellished or misremembered (as my youngest daughter would say). Some happened only in my head.

Most of the characters (all of the children) are composites of more than one person. For example, the character named "Bo" is way too much trouble to be based on just one kid. Most names have been changed to avoid unintended offense.

The following stories were previously published in whole or in part: "White Sauce," "Talkin' to Jesus," "Black Church," "Getting Some Education," "New Year's Eve," "Smitten," "Southern Man," "On the Road: Jackson, Tennessee."

CONTENTS

rock-a-hoot

new boot

chicken soup

soo goot

—call of the Barred Owl at slack tide,
as interpreted by Chief Tecumseh
Deerfoot Cook (1900–2003)

The Hollow

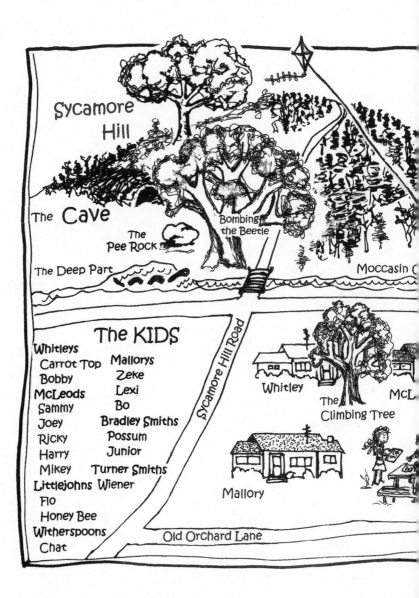

Sycamore Hill

The Cave

The Pee Rock

Bombing the Beetle

The Deep Part

Moccasin C

The KIDS

Whitleys
  Carrot Top
  Bobby
McLeods
  Sammy
  Joey
  Ricky
  Harry
  Mikey
Littlejohns
  Flo
  Honey Bee
Witherspoons
  Chat

Mallorys
  Zeke
  Lexi
  Bo
Bradley Smiths
  Possum
  Junior
Turner Smiths
  Wiener

Sycamore Hill Road

Whitley

The Climbing Tree

McL

Mallory

Old Orchard Lane

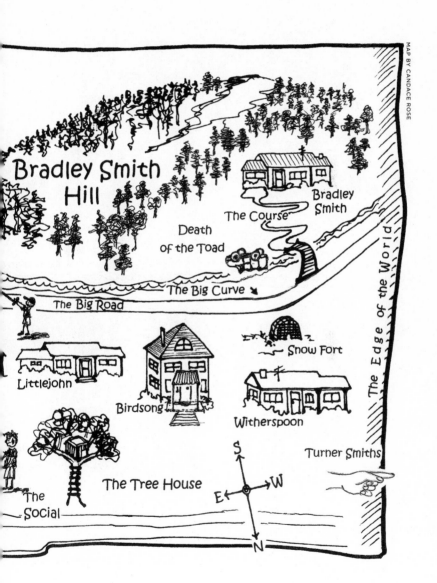

1

An Unfortunate Beginning

Several months ago, I met a couple on the sidewalk here in Walla Walla—Wendy and Roger. Wendy was a nicely tanned, blue-eyed, willowy blonde. She wore a skimpy sundress the color of yellow cake that lifted and separated her astonishingly large breasts in a pleasant sort of way, offering just a hint of tan lines.

My recollection of her doesn't leave much room for Roger. He looked pretty normal, I think.

Wendy, an avid collector of worthless information, knew that I'd written a few books. She said her husband had an amusing story and pushed Roger toward me.

"Go on, honey. Tell the nice man your story about the lobster pot."

Roger waded maybe twenty seconds into his tale before Wendy cut him off. "No, dear. That's not right. *You* leaned over the boat rail and the line tangled around *your* leg."

"No, sweetheart," Roger said. "*Harvey* was the one leaning over . . ."

Wendy shook her head. "No, sugar bear. I saw the whole thing and *you* leaned over the rail. Harvey was holding your belt."

Roger sucked up a lungful of air and rolled his eyes. "No, boopsie, you've got that backward . . ."

While they debated, the two of them wandered off.

That's all I know about the lobster pot. Not much of a story, is it? But it helps make a point: Wendy and Roger survived the lobster-pot incident (whatever it was), have undoubtedly told the story many times since, and still can't get their facts straight.

So I'm not the only one who . . .

Now that we've gotten the warnings out of the way, I can tell you these things are mostly true:

I'm a white-haired, fiftysomething guy whose double-wide Birkenstocks have disappeared from view under the bulge of his belly. I love food. When I'm not eating, I'm thinking about eating. I take exercise because my doctor won't let the subject go, not because I want to. And I've been on every diet known to man.

Until last year, I enthusiastically started a new diet each year. I did that for thirty consecutive years. Over those thirty years, I gained fifty pounds and lost a full inch of height.

What in the world is going on? I asked myself.

I talked to my wife, Annie, about it. According to Annie, Annie knows a lot of stuff. She is the guiding light of my life. (She loves it when I write things like that where other people can read them.)

I asked Annie what she thought about my weight problem. She didn't have to think. She didn't even hesitate. She rapped the kitchen table with her skinny little knuckles and said I needed therapy, lots of therapy.

This is exactly what she said: "Sam, honey, I'm begging you now. Go get yourself a good psychiatrist. Examine your portly forebears, your misspent adolescence, and your unfortunate love affair with fried chicken. Maybe there's still hope. Maybe some therapy will straighten you out."

And then she suggested that as long as I was going into therapy for my weight problem, she'd write out a list of *other issues* I could explore with my therapist, including my tendencies toward exaggeration, insensitivity, moodiness, contrariness, and—well, the list goes on.

"It's a good thing I've been keeping a list of your issues in my head," she said. "You're gonna need it."

Annie and I have been married a long time. Her list is pretty long. She's been waiting more than thirty years for an opportunity to get me fixed. I could tell she was thinking her ship had come in.

Now, just so you know, I am a good husband. I always listen to Annie's suggestions and thank her sincerely for her thoughtful advice. (She's having a little heartburn over that last sentence, but she'll get over it.)

I concluded that I wasn't up for psychotherapy. I didn't think I'd learn much lying on a sofa in a darkened room while some weirdo stared at me, took notes, and mumbled, "Hmm, that's interesting."

I told Annie what I'd decided—no therapist.

As she watched her ship head back out to sea, she shook her head and muttered under her breath, "Lordy, Lordy, Lordy."

And then, week before last, a guy-I-know suffered a mild heart attack. It wasn't anything the doctors couldn't handle, but it was enough to scare the bejesus out of him.

And me, too.

This guy-I-know was a certified butterball at the time of his infarction. His heft took his breath away, his hands swelled at temperatures above sixty-five degrees, his stomach rumbled no matter what the temperature, and his back hurt. He said he felt poorly for several weeks before the pain grabbed him by the heart and shoved him to the ground.

That got me thinking.

And then a few days later . . .

It was a glorious day. The sun hovered overhead in a cool blue sky. A frosty chill came and went on a fickle springtime breeze. It was the kind of day we McLeods call "airish."

The dogs met me at the back door, nuzzled my crotch, and slobbered on my jeans while I patted their heads. We tromped down the dusty path to the barn.

Munching on hay the color of fresh-picked turnip greens, Annie's horses eyed my pockets, thinking pleasant thoughts about carrots, or better yet, peppermint candies. Bee, our chocolate-brown mare, rotated her ears listening for the crinkle of candy wrappers as I shuffled past. Out behind the barn, Annie's alpacas lounged on a bed of fast-growing weeds and chewed their cuds, their big eyes barely visible under Lyle Lovett hairdos. BC, the barn cat, stretched out on her favorite hay bale, rolled over, and went back to sleep.

All was right with the world, except for one thing: I was feeling poorly. My brain throbbed. My back threatened to seize up. I had a bad case of indigestion and a related case of the burps. I noticed some swelling in my hands. I could go on, but you don't want to hear it.

I remembered the guy-I-know and his infarction.

So just inside the barn door, I stepped onto the scale we use to weigh the critters. A big number flashed on the screen. I didn't like it. So I stepped off, figuring that something had gone awry, and stepped back on—carefully this time.

The big number flashed again.

Alone in the barn and thinking that my barn coat, coveralls, T-shirt, and boots might be the problem, I peeled off down to my boxers. And then to make sure that I was getting the most accurate reading, I took off my glasses. And my boxers. There I stood—a mountain of pink flesh sprouting little white hairs in surprising places, all nicely accented by dark brown tan lines at my neck and wrists.

I stepped back on the scale. The number was still too big. It was a new record for me, a number pregnant with potential heart attacks and strokes.

I despaired. I sat down on a hay bale while I took it all in. Dried alfalfa blooms crunched underneath me and prodded my privates, but the discomfort didn't register. I was too deep in self-pity to notice.

I scheduled an appointment with my doctor. The nurse asked me to come in the day before for bloodletting.

I was sure my heart was failing and several veins in my head were ready to pop. Annie said I was suffering from hypochondria, but I didn't believe her. I could feel my heart swelling in my chest and blood coursing through the arteries in my neck. Everything inside me seemed to be building toward a massive heart attack, or a massive stroke, or a massive something else. I slowed down and moved deliberately so as to minimize jarring. I didn't want to stroke out before I saw my doctor.

Dr. Beauregard has been my doctor for several years now. He knows my unfortunate medical history. He knows about the grapefruit diet, and the low-carb diet, and the high-carb diet, and the melon diet, and the rice diet, and the no-rice diet, and Dr. So-and-So's diet, and Dr. Thus-and-Such's diet, the macrobiotic-something diet, body cleansings, and all the rest of it—thirty years of dieting.

Dr. Beauregard said he was pretty sure I had been on every diet ever thought up and written down. As I sat on the edge of the examining table in the paper gown that exposed more of me than it covered, Dr. Beauregard said he didn't think that my diets were working very well.

So now you know why I go to Dr. Beauregard. The man is insightful to a fault.

Surprisingly, my medical exam and blood work came out just fine. My blood pressure was a little high and my cholesterol was a little out of whack, but otherwise I checked out just fine.

Dr. Beauregard pulled his chair up a little closer to me, looked me in the eye, and said, "Sam, I'm afraid your health is pretty good. I'm afraid I've got no bad news for you. I've got no doctoral ammunition to scare you with. You could stand to lose a little weight, but without some bad news, I can't scare you into taking better care of yourself."

He didn't stop there. He went on.

"And, Sam, I'm telling you again, like I have so many times before, diets don't work. You've got to find some meaning in your life that will motivate you to take care of your body—something that gets under your skin, something that grabs your imagination, something other than a diet. And only you can figure it out."

"Meaning in my life? Like what?" I asked.

"As I said, you'll have to figure it out, Sam. I don't have any pills for that one."

The heart palpitations subsided. The veins in my head quit throbbing. Physically, I felt a little better, but emotionally I felt lost. Dr. Beauregard was not going to fix my problem for me.

Late last night, I thumbed through a well-worn romance novel somebody left lying on our sofa. It was called *Too Hot to Sleep*. Annie doesn't know where that book came from—or so she says.

As I paged through *Too Hot to Sleep* for the parts where the nubile young thing rips off her blouse to expose her tender flesh to the evident lust of her rescuer, my mind wandered. I reflected on Dr. Beauregard's advice. A few questions came to mind.

Where is the meaning in my life? What is the meaning of life it-self? What is it that'll motivate me to take better care of myself?

Darn good questions, huh? Questions I might have asked long ago. Oh well, better late than never.

I looked over to the table behind our sofa, to a framed high school photo of a much younger me standing on the shore at Old Hickory Lake outside of Nashville, Tennessee. My ribs showed above a flat stomach and my face revealed the outline of cheekbones. I realized that I had not seen my ribs or my cheekbones since I was seventeen. And then I remembered that I had not seen my penis in a while, ei-ther. As I thought about that, this is what I wrote down on the inside front cover of *Too Hot to Sleep*:

I'm off to discover meaning in my life—maybe the meaning of life itself. And when I figure it out, I'll have a reason to take better care of myself. And I'll lose some weight. And at least once before I die, I'll see my ribs again. And my cheekbones. And my penis. It's nothing to brag about but it's mine. It's been good to me. And I'd like to see it again, without the aid of a mirror, just once before I die.

I felt pretty good all of a sudden. I wasn't having heart palpita-tions and I wasn't lost anymore. I had a mission, a mission worthy of great resolve and discipline. And then I yawned and headed to bed.

So, I conceived a plan. I'm taking Annie's good advice. Well, ac-tually, just some of it. I'll revisit my deep-fried roots—the people, the places, the foods, the lessons, and the stories from my early life. I'll start at the beginning and work my way forward. Annie says all this good reflection will point me to the meaning in my life. And when I figure it out, I'll use it to take better care of myself and lose some damn weight.

Pardon my French.

BEFORE

PHOTO BY JOHN GORDON

BIG-BONED SAM

HEIGHT: 5 feet 10¾ inches

WEIGHT: 235 pounds

CLOTHING SIZE: XL (sometimes XXL)

2

Note to File

I have a new journal. It's a present from Annie. Antique brown leather, permanently bound with stitching, shiny bronze rivets, beautifully embossed, entirely handcrafted in Italy—the whole deal.

"Sam, honey, you better take notes on your road to self-discovery. Never can tell what'll be important," Annie said. "And your memory's terrible. You don't want to lose the meaning of life just because you forgot to write it down."

Good point.

So here's the first bit of bad news. I'm only an hour into this most worthy of missions, and I'm already discouraged. The voices in my head are screaming, "This'll never work, Sam. Easy to *say* you're going to discover the meaning of life. But nobody's ever *done* it. Who do you think you are?"

Good point.

"And even if you're the guy who gets it, you've got too much history under your belt, so to speak. Like your genes, and the way you came into this life, and the way you were raised. Even with the meaning of life in your back pocket, Sam, you'll never take care of yourself. You never have."

Another good point.

3

Jolley People

Not "bad" genes. Just different . . .

My genetic history is troublesome. I'm a Jolley gene carrier.

You may be familiar with it. The Jolley gene's gotten a lot of bad press recently. But if you haven't read about it, this is all you really need to know: the Jolley gene is a wonder of natural selection, a Darwinian gem; leading physicians believe it to be the most influential gene in the human genome; and, not surprisingly, its effects are easily detected.

If you doubt what I'm saying, just hop on a plane and fly off to the South (unless, of course, you're already there). Most anyplace will do. Rent a car and drive around. Find an old gas station. Ask the potbellied guys hanging out there for recommendations on the best nearby breakfast spots. They'll argue among themselves for a while. You'll have to be patient. But sooner or later they'll settle on a couple of their favorite diners.

Drive to one of them. It won't matter which one.

While you drink your coffee and peruse the menu, look around at the other customers. Keep your eyes peeled for folks who lick their lips while the waitress recites the specials. Pay particular attention to folks whose shirts are worn thin where the Formica tabletop hits them. Look for folks who go weak-kneed in the presence of ham biscuits. When you spot them, you'll have found some Jolley gene carriers.

We Jolleys think of ourselves as stout folks—solid, plump, fleshy, Rubenesque types, well positioned for the day when roundness again becomes fashionable. And while the Jolley gene gets blamed for a lot of weight-related problems, it has its good points.

As the name suggests, Jolley gene carriers are mostly happy people. We are forward-looking folks who waddle through life supported by full, gurgling bellies, thinking happy thoughts about upcoming feedings. We do not dwell on the past unless it is to reminisce about a particularly flaky piecrust or recall a satisfying helping of pot roast.

We are content with our larger-than-life selves. We Jolleys are perfectly happy to recline in our Barcaloungers and watch skinny people run to and fro. Watching skinny people fret about things—like getting to the health club before work, or whether a particular pair of pants makes them look fat, or why they didn't ask for their salad dressing on the side—provides great amusement for us Jolleys.

We take frequent naps and are therefore well rested. We nod off easily, our big heads resting comfortably on cushy double chins. We never have trouble sleeping.

And last but not least, we're surprisingly long-lived. It's rare for a Jolley to depart this life before celebrating a ninetieth birthday with a second helping of cake and a few extra scoops of homemade peach ice cream.

■   ■   ■

My mom's name is Coco. Or, at least, that's what most people call her. Coco was a Jolley long ago when she was a redheaded, freckle-faced maiden. Before she took the McLeod name.

So I, Samuel Archibald McLeod, am—underneath it all—a Jolley. The Jolley gene resides on an X chromosome somewhere in my body, probably in the vicinity of my stomach. It is a big part of who I am.

4

Big-Headed Baby Boy

Now you know why I came into this world with my mouth open. Let's examine the how . . .

It was a day so bitterly cold that metal-framed glasses stuck to the bridges of noses all over central Tennessee. The few who ventured outside watched their cloudy exhalations escape from dry, chapped lips only to disappear in a fluttering of tiny ice crystals. The sun glowed in a cloudless sky, but delivered no warmth. Mud-caked, hard-crusted snow lay in deep drifts along the icy streets.

The city of Nashville, Tennessee, barely moved, numb from the devastation of a winter storm that brought the place to its knees.

"This is a big baby," said Dr. Kettle.

"Good. Get him out of me," begged the woman who lay under a crisply starched sheet on a bare, stainless-steel delivery table.

"Wow, he's got a big head," Dr. Kettle said.

"I know," cried Coco.

"And he's got a set of lungs on him, too," said Dr. Kettle. "I think the boy's hungry."

"Just my luck," said Coco.

February 5, 1951: it was a good day to be born.

Not much has ever happened on February 5. It is a particularly benign date. Nineteen hundred and fifty-one was also a fairly benign year. Most of our world was resting up from World War II. Koreans were still killing each other but most everybody else was taking a breather. In fact, even here in These United States, we didn't kill each other as much during the 1950s as we do today—a mere 4.9 homicides per 100,000 in 1951 versus 5.6 homicides per 100,000 today.

Unfortunately, we Americans were a lot more accident-prone back then—roughly sixty accidental deaths per 100,000 in the 1950s compared with thirty-five or so per 100,000 today. We regularly smashed up our cars, fell off of sidewalks into oncoming traffic, and slipped on stuff in grocery stores.

The year 1951 is best remembered in my hometown—Nashville, Tennessee—as the year of the Great Blizzard, a horrific storm that came barreling in on January 29 and didn't move on until February 1.

On February 5, the day of my birth, automobiles still littered ditches along roadways, thousands of trees lay across power lines, planes that had been grounded for days taxied icy runways seeking a way out, and rapidly melting ice threatened massive floods.

Hungry Nashvillians made their way, mostly on foot, to grocery stores in search of sustenance—particularly eggs, milk, and bread—things we Nashvillians ate in moderation most of the time but got some sort of collective craving for whenever there was a snowstorm.

So, depending upon your perspective, February 5, 1951, was the tail end of devastation and inconvenience or the beginning of recovery, hope, and rebuilding. I prefer to think of my birth date as the latter.

I have heard several versions of the following story, which is one of those walked-ten-miles-to-school-each-way-every-day-in-snowshoes tales:

Coco, whose memory is, according to her, still pretty sharp, says that she and my dad struck out for Vanderbilt Hospital on the evening of February 4, when she and I went into labor. Ice covered the streets at least a foot deep. Snowdrifts blanketed abandoned cars. Fierce gusts menaced our car as we poked along.

(Research doesn't support Mom's claims, but, hey, her version of the story is a lot more exciting.)

There are conflicting reports on this next part. Coco says Dad could have docked our Chevy at the foot of the hospital steps, making her trek in the snow much shorter, while Dad says the ice was so treacherous that he'd have been nuts to try pulling up there.

Suffice it to say that on the way from the car to the hospital entrance, one of those accidents that were rampant in the 1950s befell my mom. The stork had dropped me into an accident-prone woman. Coco took a tumble into a deep snowdrift, where the two of us lay until Dad, who was a doctor and had a bit of influence, summoned a bunch of orderlies to hoist us back to our feet.

Thankfully, our accident was not one of the sixty per 100,000 that resulted in somebody's death, but it did hasten my delivery and resulted in a badly sprained ankle for Coco—an ankle that, to this day, throbs a bit every February 5 as a reminder of my arrival.

5

Belly Up to the Training Table

From my first day on this planet, hunger has been my constant, whining companion . . .

Following my arrival, four younger brothers showed up in quick succession—Joey, Ricky, Harry, and Mikey. Coco delivered all five of us in the short span of seven years. She tried to get a girl baby, but after the birth of the fifth boy, she said "to hell with it" and gave up.

That was a good decision. Five boys were a handful. The place was bedlam, except at feedings, when fisticuffs were suspended in favor of taking on fuel. The brief calm around meals encouraged Coco to feed us regularly and often.

Coco's table was round, seated eight comfortably, and sported a fast-spinning lazy Susan. Our world revolved around that table.

Next to the table, in a corner, pushed up against the pine-paneled wall, was a green-painted two-drawer chest. I don't know what was in it—I don't reckon I ever looked—but on top of that chest sat a milk-dispensing refrigerator that held two five-gallon cartons of whole milk, replaced every week by Barney, the milkman.

We consumed ten gallons of frothy, cold milk every week. That's two gallons per boy per week, or 104 gallons per boy per year, or 1,664 glasses of milk per boy per year, or 4.7 glasses of milk per boy per day—on average. And that doesn't include the milk we drank at school.

An eight-ounce glass of whole milk contains about 4 percent milk fat—good, wholesome, nonhydrogenated milk fat. I won't bore you with more arithmetic, but that means each of us boys consumed four gallons of milk fat per year. The Jolley gene was happy.

We also liked Krispy Kreme donuts. As Barney pulled out of our driveway, the donut man often pulled in. His name was Roy. He delivered ten dozen plain glazed donuts to our house every two weeks. Again, I won't bore you with the math, but if you were to do the calculations you'd find that each of us ate 1.7 donuts a day on average—about six hundred Krispy Creme donuts per boy per year.

In addition to donuts, we ate scrambled eggs. And we ate bacon—lots of bacon. It makes my heart hurt to think about how much bacon we ate every day—four to five pieces wouldn't be far off the mark. And our eggs were scrambled in bacon fat.

We had toast—well-buttered Wonder bread toast—slathered with homemade fig preserves or Welch's grape jelly. And grits—yummy cheese grits. Mom made the best cheese grits you ever tasted, with plenty of butter, salt, and Cheddar cheese.

Coco used real butter until oleomargarine came onto the market. It was supposed to be the healthy alternative to butter and was made with hydrogenated vegetable oil—the silent killer that filled deep-fat fryers all over These United States until recently, when public health officials scared us back to butter.

You might say Coco was a darn good short-order cook who, like her mother before her, spent the better part of every day in the kitchen, busier than a stump-tailed cow in fly time. After serving up a massive breakfast, she'd start in on our sack lunches—a couple of tuna salad sandwiches on white bread with the crusts cut off, chips or Fritos, a big bagful of Oreo cookies, and some sweet pickles. We each got a dime to take with us to school so we could buy a carton of milk and a brick of hard-frozen butter-brickle ice cream to go with our Oreos. Ten cents was a lot of money back in the good ol' days.

And once the sack lunches were lined up on the kitchen counter, she started cooking turnip greens in a huge pressure cooker, generously seasoned with salt and bacon fat to make them go down easier.

By dinnertime, the lazy Susan was piled high: Coco's meatloaf, a great mound of mashed potatoes, a big bowl of buttered green peas, fatted turnip greens, buttered dinner rolls, and applesauce—a quart jar of applesauce. Back in those days, applesauce didn't come au naturel; it came with a truckload of refined sugar mixed in so it'd be nice and sweet. And if we cleaned our plates, there was dessert. One of our favorites was Hostess cake shells filled to overflowing with sugarcoated strawberries topped with a spluttering of Reddi-wip. "Made with real cream," the can says, "and propellants."

We washed it all down with a couple of the 4.7 glasses of milk we were encouraged to drink each day. "Drink your milk," Coco said. "It'll make your bones strong." She left out the part about heart attacks.

An hour or so after dinner, we ate a few more Oreo cookies, drank another glass of milk, brushed our teeth, and went to bed. Coco cleaned up the kitchen and got another dozen Krispy Kreme donuts out of the freezer to thaw before breakfast.

In the midst of chaos, Coco's meatloaf rested unadorned on an oval-shaped white plastic platter in the middle of the lazy Susan. Its aroma filled the house, offering comfort and constancy. It made me lick my lips. It made my knees feel wobbly. And it tasted good, too.

Now, I know your mom makes good meatloaf; almost everybody's mom does. (Our neighbor Mrs. Littlejohn didn't, and probably still doesn't, but she is an unusual case. More about her later.)

Anyway, Coco makes *really* good meatloaf—juicy and beefy. And ketchup is the perfect topping. Even Coco agrees that her meatloaf is better with a generous squirt of ketchup.

So, on the off chance that you're willing to try somebody else's meatloaf, I've included the recipe here just for you.

Coco's Meatloaf

Serves 8

Ingredients

¾ cup chopped yellow onion

½ cup chopped green bell pepper

¼ cup milk

¼ cup ketchup

2 eggs

2 cups crushed saltine crackers

2 pounds ground beef

2 teaspoons kosher salt

1 teaspoon dry mustard

PREHEAT oven to 400°.

PLACE the first five ingredients in a blender and blend until smooth.

PUT the remaining ingredients in a large bowl, add the contents of the blender, and lightly combine.

MOVE the contents of the bowl to a shallow baking dish and shape the mixture into a loaf. Decorate the top of the meatloaf with a couple of tablespoons of ketchup. (Let your creative juices flow.)

BAKE for one hour.

REMOVE the meatloaf from the oven and allow it to rest uncovered for fifteen minutes.

SLICE and serve—preferably with a big bottle of ketchup close by. Get ready for a life-changing experience.

6

Getting Some Manners

A Coco rule: If you're going to eat a lot, you must look good doing it . . .

There came a time when Coco decided that we needed to get some manners. She was appalled at our dinnertime feeding frenzies. Used to them, but appalled.

Coco believed that eating in restaurants from time to time would encourage better behavior. Restaurants would provide an atmosphere conducive to learning knife-and-fork etiquette. Her belief lacked logic, but had plenty of enthusiasm behind it. Dad was skeptical, but not sufficiently hostile to the idea to save us from Coco's folly.

On most Sunday mornings, we McLeods went off to Sunday school followed by the main church service, what we called "Big Church." We escaped a few minutes after noon, and on the way to the Toad—our name for Coco's lime-green 1954 Ford Country Squire station wagon with the fake wood paneling—we ripped the clip-on ties from our button-down shirt collars and flung our sport coats onto the floorboards.

That was the drill on most Sunday mornings.

But after Coco got her wild hair about getting us some manners, the Sunday routine changed. Coco threatened to strip us naked in front of girls and hang us from the nearest tree if we touched our ties or even thought about taking off our coats, because we were headed to Cross Keys—a fancy downtown restaurant—for Sunday lunch and some training in civility.

We sat at a dimly lit table near the restrooms at the back of the restaurant—our regular table, where Grayson, the guy with the menus, figured we'd blend into the activity around the kitchen door and not disturb the civilized guests nearer the front of the restaurant. He was mostly right.

Cross Keys was best known for the extra-large basket of cornbread sticks that our waitress, Donna, delivered to the table within seconds of our arrival. As Donna set the basket on the table, Coco ordered each of us boys a fried-chicken plate, the Cross Keys salad for herself, and calf's liver smothered in onions for Dad, even though Donna already knew what we were having. Delays in getting food on the table were not good. Donna and Coco understood that.

Before our lunch arrived, we could easily down three or four baskets of the cornbread sticks while Coco repeated her well-rehearsed line, "Don't eat any more of that corn bread, boys. You'll ruin your appetites."

We were instructed to place our napkins in our laps, where they could more easily fall on the floor. This meant that, at any one time, there were more of us crawling on the carpet retrieving napkins than there were sitting at the table.

Dad pushed back a bit from the table so as to avoid the melee.

On one particularly memorable Sunday, Mikey toddled out from under our table and made a beeline for a well-lit table near the front of the restaurant where he cajoled some blue-hairs into giving him several cornbread sticks before Coco caught him. Meanwhile, Harry spilled his water on Joey. Joey punched Harry. Harry hollered like a scalded beagle. Ricky said he had to go to the bathroom, hung on to the tablecloth as he climbed down from his chair, and damn near pulled the entire table setting onto his head while Mikey toddled off again.

I was the only angel among us—a model boy happily eating another cornbread stick dredged in butter.

Fried chicken was one of our favorites—hot, crispy, and delicious. Coco's fried chicken was the best, but we were willing to eat somebody else's. I'm sure the Cross Keys fried chicken came with potatoes—probably mashed—and a vegetable or two, but I have no recollection of it. With the chicken came a brimming basket of hot, sticky-sweet cinnamon rolls—the kind with buttery soft centers dripping warm icing. And that's what we ate—fried chicken and cinnamon rolls—while my dad picked at his liver, pushed a little farther from the table, and hid his face in his napkin.

By the time we lay back in our chairs completely sated, we were an ugly mess—our faces, hands, shirts, and ties splattered with Crisco from the fried chicken and cinnamon-laced butter from the buns. Coco, who never put her napkin in her lap and never used her napkin to wipe her own mouth, unceremoniously dunked it in her glass of water, got out of her chair, and went around the table giving each of us the once-over.

By now my dad was so far from our table that he appeared to be seated with the folks at the next table, which was exactly the impression he was trying to promote.

After our birdbath, we marched back out to the Toad, rumpled messes and only slightly better mannered. Back home, Coco took to her bed for the afternoon. Getting us manners was hard work.

7

Another Note to File

That was sort of depressing, wasn't it? Genetic challenges, formative years fueled by fat, the table manners of a Viking. I don't know what to say except it's NOT MY FAULT.

I talked to Annie about my unfortunate upbringing—again. She shook her head longer than necessary and said, "Sam, honey, this isn't that hard. You've got the whole thing ass backward in your head. Forget about losing weight. Focus on the lessons in those stories. It'll consume your meager brainpower, leaving you no wattage to waste on your weight obsession."

"But . . ." I started while she climbed up on her soapbox, stood on her tiptoes, and wagged her finger at me.

"Don't push it," she preached. "If you open your mind and allow the meaning of life to come to you, instead of beating the subject hammer and tong, doors will open and answers will come, and the weight thing will take care of itself. I promise."

How the hell Annie knows these things is beyond me. She says only women have the emotional intelligence necessary to divine fundamental truths and that's why it's a damn good thing I'm married to her, and why I should pay more attention to what she says, and why . . .

8

Gimme a Ticket for an Aeroplane

Good things come in small envelopes.

The envelope was sky blue, tiny, and addressed to: Sam McLeod, Walla Walla, Washington.

No street address. No post office box. No zip code. No return address.

The card inside said:

A Neighborhood Social
Noon to 6:00 PM Saturday, May 17, 2009
The Mallorys' Backyard
Rain or Shine. No RSVP. No Excuses.

Annie, hovering over my right shoulder, read along with me.

"Lexi," she said.

"What?"

"Lexi," Annie repeated, crossing her arms over her chest. "Your childhood sweetheart. Coco told me all about her. Said she was stuck on you. I wondered if you'd ever hear from her."

"Hear from Lexi? The girl from my old neighborhood? The place where I grew up? You think this is from Lexi?"

"She's no girl anymore, Sam. She's a woman," Annie said.

"She wasn't my girlfriend," I said.

"That's what you think," Annie replied, stroking her chin, tapping her cheek with her index finger. "You men are all the same," she added, as if that explained something.

"Well, how'd she find me?" I asked.

"I don't know," said Annie, still puzzling over the mystery.

"I wasn't her boyfriend," I said. "Just her friend."

Annie shook her head and muttered, "Lordy, Lordy, Lordy."

A few days later . . .

"I've decided not to go to the social," I told Annie. "It's too far. The trip'll cost too much. Airline prices are ridiculous these days. And traveling east of the Mississippi? People everywhere. I won't be able to handle it. Plus I don't have enough time to lose more than a few pounds. I need time to get in shape. This thing is just a couple of weeks away. There's no time to plan the trip. There's—"

"Sam," Annie interrupted. "Here's a map and your itinerary. You're driving. It's all laid out for you. You leave here one week from today and spend the first night in Missoula with Summer and Rusty. Next night in Buffalo, Wyoming. You're staying at the Occidental, the old hotel you like so much. Then to Nebraska. You can stop wherever you want. There are Holiday Inns all along the highway. Alice and Charlie are expecting you in Columbia, Missouri, on the fourteenth. Alice says she's baking your favorite apple pie."

"The one with the Cheddar cheese?"

"Yes, the one with the Cheddar cheese. The next night, you're having dinner with Wiese in Jackson. Then a full day at the farm on the sixteenth with your Aunt Irma and Uncle Pete. On to Nashville on the seventeenth, arriving in time for the social. Your mom will meet you there. Mike and Harry are coming, too. It's all set."

"But—" I started.

"No more buts, Sam. A lot of people, including yours truly, have worked hard to make this happen for you. You're supposed to take this trip. I've been thinking about this a lot, letting my superior emotional intelligence work on it. This is a door opening. You need to get back to Nashville before it closes. I'll take care of things here at the farm. But you keep you hands off that old girlfriend, you hear me?

"Oh, almost forgot, you've got an appointment at eight o'clock tomorrow morning to get the oil changed in your car."

Annie saw confusion wobbling around on my chubby cheeks.

"Sam, honey"—her voice went soft—"you're going to enjoy this trip. You're going to see your old neighborhood and old friends. You're going to learn something important. I'm sure of it."

She kissed me on the cheek.

"But—"

"No more buts, Sam."

9

A Cast of Characters

The old neighborhood, I remember it well . . .

My world was a peaceful place—a small valley west of Nashville called Jocelyn Hollow.

I say "peaceful" because natural disasters around the Hollow didn't amount to much. Denizens still remember the twenty-foot sinkhole in the Mallorys' front yard that destroyed their septic tank, causing you-know-what to run out all over the place, stinking up the neighborhood but fertilizing yards up and down Old Orchard Lane, making them the prettiest, greenest things you ever did see.

There was the time a buzzard fell dead from fifty feet up in the oak tree in the Whitleys' backyard and bonked Wiener Turner Smith on the head. Knocked him out cold. He came to when Mrs. Whitley, who'd been sunning herself on the porch, ran across the yard in her green bathing suit with the rubber daisies down the side and tossed a tumblerful of iced tea in Wiener's face. Dr. Pritchard said Wiener suffered a mild concussion and would be none the worse for wear, but later we found out the incident instilled in Wiener a powerful fear of buzzards.

Those were the kinds of natural disasters we dealt with in the Hollow.

There were no wars or serious altercations. But there was the time Mrs. Littlejohn, haphazardly wrapped in a blue-striped towel and still dripping from the shower, answered her front door thinking her new patio furniture had finally arrived (she'd been waiting two whole weeks), only to find Jimmy Whitworth, the newspaper boy, standing there with *The Nashville Tennessean* in one hand and a bill in the other, staring at her chest. Well, she grabbed that rolled-up newspaper and damned near beat Jimmy to death with it, mad at him for not being the patio furniture deliveryman *and* for getting her out of the shower before she'd had a chance to shampoo *and* for shooting her a lascivious look. At least that's what she called it.

No, the Hollow was not the kind of place you read about in *The Nashville Tennessean*. In fact, we rarely knew anybody who got his name in the paper. Chat Witherspoon once knew somebody who knew somebody who got her name in the paper for running her car through the front window of Beasley Hardware without killing anybody, and Lexi Mallory and her brother Zeke got their pictures in the paper standing outside the new Krispy Kreme donut shop at the grand opening. But that's about as close as we ever got to fame.

When we McLeods moved into the Hollow, our four-bedroom, two-bath, redbrick rancher stood alone in a two-acre sea of dandelions—no trees or shrubs to amount to anything. On summer afternoons we hustled after dust devils swirling across our yard, blowing up great clouds of dandelion seeds and floating them over to the neighbors'.

Sometimes the air was so full of dandelion seeds we couldn't breathe without getting them up our noses. Possum Bradley Smith got one way up his snoot, and bugs went to town on it like it was a picnic lunch. Before it was over, Dr. Pritchard had to go in there with a scraper and get the thing out. Possum ended up looking like he'd been beaten about the head with a stick. Not pretty.

Densely wooded hills peppered with limestone caves and laced with free-flowing springs surrounded us. The springs were home to blaze-orange salamanders, thumb-size minnows, freshwater crawdads, and the occasional water moccasin. The prospect of treading on deadly poisonous snakes made the place sort of interesting.

Moccasin Creek collected the water that flowed from the springs and ran right down the middle of our valley. It was named after Big 'Un, as in "You best watch out for that reptile; he's a big 'un"—a gray-black water moccasin sighted occasionally along the creek bank. While none of us ever saw all of him, folks claimed he was as long as two kids stitched together head to head and as fat as a family-size can of Franco-American spaghetti. Word of a Big 'Un sighting spread faster than the mumps and served notice to kids from other neighborhoods that they'd best stay clear of our stomping ground.

Moccasin Creek was deep enough for swimming in a few spots and generally suitable for damming, wading, sailing stick-boats, and fishing for suckers with dough balls. Drowning was possible but challenging.

The Big Road was a little-traveled, mostly gravel lane that wound its way down valley. And while our moms warned us to look both ways before crossing it, we were more likely to get hit by a hay wagon than a car. Flo Littlejohn went running across it one day. Mrs. Whitley, who was spraying the handrails on her porch with Lysol, saw her and hollered at her to walk, not run. Said she might get hurt. Which she did when she twisted her head around to see Mrs. Whitley instead of looking where she was going, missed her next step, took a nosedive into the gravel, lost two teeth, scraped the skin off both kneecaps, and broke her ankle. She was the first kid in the neighborhood to get crutches and enjoyed some brief celebrity.

Across the Big Road, rising up from Moccasin Creek, was Sycamore Hill, the neighborhood playground. It was chockablock with mossy oak, big-flower tulip, towering sycamore, Osage orange, and sharp-needled fir trees. Grapevines hung like ropes from the treetops. On one well-worn stretch of hillside, a reasonably coordinated kid could swing Tarzan-like on four vines without touching the ground, landing in the Deep Part of Moccasin Creek—the best swimming hole in the valley unless Big 'Un happened to be hanging out there sharpening his fangs.

Just uphill from the Deep Part was the Cave, a limestone cavern sunk deep into the hillside's loose, loamy soil—a hole in the ground easily overlooked by the occasional hiker but big enough to house four or five kids at one time, if a couple of us sat on the ledge near the back of the Cave. The ledge hung out over a room-size cavern, accessed by a rope that hung ten feet to the cavern's floor—a room we called the Number Two Room, not because it was the second room in the Cave, but because Carrot Top took a dump there one day when his brother, Bobby, pulled the rope up and *left him there to rot*—or words to that effect.

A whole gaggle of brown bats lived in the Number Two Room. They didn't suck blood but scared the pants off anybody wandering the hillside at dusk when they blew out of the Cave in a dark cloud of high-pitched squeaking. They also used the Number Two Room as a bathroom, so Carrot Top didn't really add much to the guano that already covered the cavern floor.

To the west of Sycamore Hill was another slightly smaller hill, but steeper. The Bradley Smiths lived at the top of it. We called them the Bradley Smiths to separate them in our minds from the Turner Smiths, who lived farther up the Hollow but close enough to the Bradley Smiths to cause confusion.

Getting to the Bradley Smiths' house from the Big Road involved a considerable hike on short legs up their paved and winding driveway, which was so steep that none of us kids could ride a bike all the way to the top. On snow days, the Bradley Smiths' driveway turned into the Course, a sled run so treacherous that only big kids were permitted on it and even they often went off course and made an unplanned trip to the emergency room to get put back together by Dr. Pritchard.

Perry "Possum" Bradley Smith and his twin brother, Bradley "Junior" Bradley Smith, lived up there. Had they not owned the Course, I doubt we'd have counted them as neighborhood kids. They were nice enough, but getting up that hill was a serious impediment to relationship development. We McLeods didn't normally go up there unless Coco drove us in the Toad.

Possum was short, square-shouldered, blond, and beady-eyed. "Built like a brick shithouse with a flat roof," Granddaddy McLeod said. When injured, Possum whined until he realized he wasn't getting the attention he deserved, and then played dead. Junior didn't look at all like Possum and was not a faker. He was tall, skinny, dark-skinned, and fat-lipped. Even with his mouth closed, his lips looked like a wad of Dubble Bubble stuck up under his nose. Because of the differences in their looks, nobody ever referred to the boys as the "Bradley Smith twins." Doing so invited wonder and bogged down conversation in tiresome speculation.

Mrs. Bradley Smith fancied herself a Lauren Bacall look-alike even though she was short and plain, not tall and glamorous. There was no doubt she was Possum's mom. She talked funny on the phone, calling folks "dah-lin'." And she chain-smoked Benson & Hedges Superslims through a foot-long black onyx cigarette holder while she made notes to herself and checked her calendars.

Organization was not Mrs. Bradley Smith's strong suit. She wrote notes to herself on everything—the backs of unopened bills, grocery-store receipts, the telephone book, and the calendar on the refrigerator. When she wasn't writing a note, she was searching for one. Always saying, "I know I wrote that down somewhere."

She kept at least three calendars—one beside each phone in the house—but rarely coordinated them. It never occurred to her that her system was flawed, and nobody was brave enough to tell her. As a consequence, the Bradley Smiths were famously unreliable when it came to appointments.

The pink brick house at the corner of the Big Road and Sycamore Hill was home to the Whitley boys, Bobby and Carrot Top. They were redheads—way more redheaded than my mom—and so generously freckled that there was hardly any regular skin on them. Bobby had a cowlick above his forehead that looked like the swirl in a milkshake blender.

Carrot Top, four years older than Bobby, did enough bizarre stuff before Bobby arrived on this earth to earn a reputation for daring and stupidity. If a stunt was life threatening and therefore not worth considering, Carrot Top would do it, survive it, and on average get about twenty stitches for it. He had more scars on his body than anybody could count—damn near more scars than freckles.

"Poor little Bobby," as we all called him, suffered from arriving in this world after Carrot Top. By the time he came along, Mrs. Whitley, a petite brunette prone to wearing lime-green pedal pushers, hot-pink blouses, and matching pink heels, was slightly deranged from Carrot Top's living on the edge and regularly stumbling over it. She seemed resigned to Carrot Top's near-certain childhood death and dealt with his impending doom by hovering over little Bobby's every move, ready to protect him from any brush with boyhood. She toted a can of Lysol around with her, spraying and wiping surfaces while she lectured Bobby on the dangers he faced. Once she caught us kids, including Bobby, poking sticks at a hornets' nest in the bushes by their screened porch. She raced into the yard screaming, grabbed Bobby, sprayed the hornets buzzing around him with Lysol, and ducked back into the house. She left the rest of us, including Carrot Top, to fend for ourselves.

As a consequence of Mrs. Whitley's neurotic overprotectiveness, Bobby rarely did much with us, and when he did, got teased so unmercifully that he'd lash out and do something like strand his brother in the Number Two Room, where he'd be forced to take his infamous dump.

Mr. and Mrs. Birdsong lived a couple of houses west of us, between the Littlejohns and the Witherspoons. They were old, really old, and, like my grandparents, sat out on their front porch most nights in the summertime. Mrs. Birdsong was a tiny woman with white hair and faded blue eyes who shelled a lot of peas and kept a bowl of brightly wrapped hard candies on the table by the front door. There weren't many days when we kids missed a stop at the Birdsongs', where Mrs. Birdsong quizzed us for family news while she doled out the candy.

When he wasn't helping a neighborhood mom with a leaky faucet, Mr. Birdsong could be found on his back porch making a piece of furniture and eyeing their freestanding garage as possible expansion space. Mrs. Birdsong said, "Over my dead body." And she meant it.

Unfortunately she died soon thereafter—near the end of 1957. It was a great shock to all of us, including Mr. Birdsong. While he grieved, he moved his woodworking tools into the garage.

Flo and Honey Bee Littlejohn lived next door—between us McLeods and the Birdsongs. Honey Bee was not really a neighborhood kid. She, like Bobby Whitley, never did much with the rest of us. Near as I could tell, Honey Bee was born wearing a red party dress, lots of jingly bracelets, black patent-leather shoes, and a big-bowed hair ribbon. She looked a lot like her mom. And her mom always looked like she was headed to a cocktail party.

Honey Bee cared for her extended family of dolls (four generations including great-aunts and distant cousins) with studied efficiency.

She knew who was related to whom, which of the cousins had just had her tonsils out, and all about Uncle Harry's bout with gout. She posed her little darlings just so on metal-framed twin beds clothed in pristine white bedspreads. On the rare occasion when I was thrown in with her and got around to playing some game, Honey Bee invariably suggested we play Family or School or House—games that involved moving dolls (under Honey Bee's supervision) around in the dollhouse mansions that lined the wall beneath her bedroom's bay window. Honey Bee had little tolerance for child-rearing mistakes, especially from the likes of me. As potential husband material, I languished at the bottom of Honey's list.

Fine by me.

Flo, on the other hand, was part girl and part tomboy. She could play dolls with Honey Bee and Kick-the-Can with the rest of us. She often hung out with Mr. Birdsong and helped him with his woodworking projects. She had an appreciable talent for sanding newly made furniture and oiling it to a fine finish. Kids who were having relationship issues went to Flo for advice. She was wise beyond her years when it came to interpersonal skills.

Mrs. Littlejohn wore high heels, brightly colored hair ribbons in her bleached-blonde hair, and party dresses, while she vacuumed. She loved to vacuum, but when the vacuuming was done; she mostly lay around in her bikini on a flowery-cushioned lounge chair in her backyard while her maid cooked and cleaned. Mrs. Littlejohn was not into tan lines. Her bikini top was therefore more off than on. That was nice for us boys, who wouldn't have known much about boobs had it not been for Mrs. Littlejohn.

The Mallorys lived up behind us, their split-level, brick-and-cedar-sided house facing onto Old Orchard Lane. Zeke, the oldest of the three Mallory kids, was a year older than me. He wore heavy black-framed glasses so thick he appeared to be staring at you from some other place. He was an Erector-set kind of guy and rarely left the basement of the Mallorys' house, a nerd long before the term was coined.

Lexi, who may be the brains behind the upcoming social, came next in the Mallory lineup and was a girl, but barely. She wasn't at all like Honey Bee, and went way past Flo on the tomboy scale. She rubber-banded her flaxen curly hair into a permanent ponytail, wore Red Ball Jet high-top tennis shoes, peed in the woods, and could swing on a grapevine like a lemur. She did everything with us boys and was not somebody to mess with when she put on her mean look.

Bo, Lexi's weird little brother, was forever wandering off, causing the neighborhood moms to mobilize well-rehearsed but poorly executed search-and-rescue missions. Bo thought he was a dog most of the time and chased the milk truck up and down the Mallorys' driveway.

And if you did something to make Bo mad, he'd get you back by peeing on your leg while you weren't looking. Urinating was Bo's principal means of fighting back. Sometimes he'd set your yard on fire, but mostly he just peed on folks. Happily, he was over most of this by the time he turned five.

Keeping up with Bo was Mrs. Mallory's cross to bear. Her face was so lined with worry that the bald spot on top of her head was hardly noticeable. To cover it, she wore scarves until somebody said she looked like the old maid in a card deck. According to Mrs. Whitley, Mrs. Mallory was going to fret herself into a wig if she didn't pack her budding juvenile delinquent off to reform school where he belonged. (Mrs. Whitley conveniently overlooked the fact that her boy Carrot Top had taught Bo most everything he knew.)

The Mallorys had a huge tree house in an old oak in their backyard. Mr. Mallory and Mr. Birdsong built it one weekend with our help. We sawed boards on the electric table saw in Mr. Mallory's shop. We hammered a lot. Mr. Birdsong brought a bunch of his woodworking tools and showed us kids how to use them: a plane for shaving off rough edges, a level to check to see if things were out of kilter, and a hand drill for drilling out peepholes so we could spy on the neighborhood.

That tree house was no makeshift affair. And to top it all off, we painted the thing Day-Glo orange. The Mallorys' tree house was visible from almost anywhere in the Hollow.

The Witherspoons lived beyond the Birdsongs at the Big Curve in the Big Road. Chattanooga (or "Chat") was my best friend. A year older than me, Chat exhibited the wisdom of an elder and, unlike Carrot Top, Possum, or Junior, hardly ever told me to do anything really stupid. I was the kind of kid who did what older kids told me to do. As a result, I did a lot of stupid things. I guess that's why I liked Chat so much.

Chat got his cool from his mom. Like Coco, Mrs. Witherspoon was one of the more levelheaded ladies in the neighborhood. In the midst of a crisis, she was still-water calm and had a way of reeling in jumpier moms to keep them from exacerbating the problem, whatever it was. An accomplished storyteller, Mrs. Witherspoon spent Friday evenings on the screened back porch reading to us kids while Mr. Witherspoon was off playing poker. When the mood took her, she'd close the book she was reading and make up the rest of the story in her head. She and my Granddaddy McLeod were the best storytellers I knew.

Last but by no means least, there was Wiener, who was the Turner Smiths' boy, and like I said, deathly afraid of buzzards. The Turner Smiths lived beyond the edge of the world as I knew it, way up valley. Wiener Turner Smith arrived in our world on foot, by bike, or in the backseat of his mother's car. One day Mrs. Turner Smith had a minor accident driving down the Big Road while simultaneously trying to get Wiener's finger out of the cigarette lighter where it had somehow gotten stuck. Mrs. Turner Smith, who was what you might call excitable, ran off the Big Road, mowed down the Birdsongs' hedge, and lost the front bumper on her car. From that day forward, Wiener was not allowed to ride in the front seat and was prohibited from sticking his finger in anything.

Come to think of it, Wiener often got some part of himself stuck in something. His real name was Courtney, a name he hated, so he was always encouraging us to give him a neat nickname, which we did when one day he got his wiener caught in the zipper of his pants up in the Mallorys' tree house. He never told anybody how that happened but he did come screaming down out of that tree begging somebody to get him unstuck, which we boys were not about to do but which Lexi did without complaint. He ran, with his little thing bleeding, all the way home, and ended up taking a trip to see Dr. Pritchard. He healed, but from that day forward he was Wiener.

Every Labor Day—generally the hottest, most humid day of the entire summer—the Hollow held a social. That's what the moms called it; it was really just a picnic.

Coco made fried chicken, pimento cheese sandwiches, and her tangy marinated vegetables. Mrs. Mallory brought her deviled eggs and ginger ale salad. Mrs. Turner Smith also brought deviled eggs.

Demand for deviled eggs was high. It galled Mrs. Turner Smith that Mrs. Mallory's deviled eggs disappeared first, but that didn't keep her from bringing her own, constantly tweaking her recipe to see if she could take the high ground from Mrs. Mallory. One year Mrs. Turner Smith announced that she'd hidden a brand-new, shiny penny in one of her deviled eggs and whoever found it would win a prize: a glider with a propeller powered by a fat rubber band. And sure enough, her deviled eggs went first—until Junior bit down on that penny so hard that he broke a molar. And swallowed the molar. And the penny. That sent the Bradley Smiths off to the dentist and the rest of us back to the plate of Mrs. Mallory's deviled eggs.

Mrs. Mallory's ginger ale salad was also a neighborhood favorite and the centerpiece of any social. It sat in the middle of the table full of maraschino cherries, looking for all the world like a picture on the Candy Land board. You might want to give it a try.

Mrs. Mallory's Ginger Ale Salad

Serves 8

Ingredients

2 envelopes (¼ oz. each) unflavored gelatin

⅓ cup cold water

1 can (8 oz.) crushed pineapple in its juice

1½ cups ginger ale (the best you can find)

1 jar (10 oz.) maraschino cherries, drained

iceberg lettuce leaves to cover a serving platter

IN a medium bowl, soften the gelatin in the water.

IN a small saucepan, bring the crushed pineapple (and its juice) to a simmer.

POUR the simmering pineapple over the softened gelatin and stir until the gelatin is completely dissolved. Add the ginger ale and cherries. (The flavor of the ginger ale makes this dish, so buy the most flavorful ginger ale you can find.)

POUR the mixture into a small mold and refrigerate until set—two to three hours.

REMOVE the mold from the refrigerator. Dip the mold in a warm-water bath and un-mold the Ginger Ale Salad onto a serving platter covered with iceberg lettuce leaves.

ADMIRE its beauty for a while before serving.

■　　■　　■

Sodas, paper plates, napkins, and plastic forks were supplied by Mrs. Littlejohn, who wasn't much of a cook. As you know, the woman couldn't even make a decent meatloaf. At one memorable social held in the Littlejohns' backyard, she served dry sandwiches of American cheese on white bread. No mayonnaise, mustard, or butter. She didn't even cut the crusts off the bread. Next to the platter of sandwiches sat a large bowl of soggy potato chips she'd refrigerated so they'd be "refreshing." That was the last time Mrs. Littlejohn was asked to bring a food dish to a social.

Mrs. Birdsong did pies: lemon meringue, chocolate chess, strawberry, apple, peach and cherry (a perennial favorite). The lady could bake. Until she died, nobody ever left a social thinking they hadn't had enough pie. When Mrs. Birdsong went on to Heaven Above, not only did she leave us without pie, but Mrs. Littlejohn seized on the opportunity to bring desserts to our socials—mostly Oreos and Fig Newtons from the bag. That was okay, but we all missed pie.

Mrs. Witherspoon always brought a fruit salad and ham biscuits—not country ham biscuits, just regular old ham biscuits that were acceptable but not really what anybody was hoping for.

Mrs. Bradley Smith did a pickle tray and green-tomato pie—most of the time. She sometimes forgot the pickles but never forgot the tomato pie. It was a big winner. She couldn't make enough to satisfy her fans.

Mrs. Whitley, who was a worrywart of the first order, brought bananas and individually wrapped cupcakes so her Bobby would have something to eat that wouldn't expose him to neighborhood germs. Once, Wiener sneaked several of Mrs. Mallory's deviled eggs to Bobby. When Mrs. Whitley caught him with a mouthful of masticated egg, she flew completely off the handle, jerked Bobby off his picnic bench, sprayed him head to toe with Lysol, and hauled him home for a bath. Mrs. Whitley could be a little wacky, but that performance took the cake (so to speak).

10

No Messin' with My Vidalias

And it wasn't just neighborhood socials that stirred culinary juices in the moms . . .

We sat at the table eating our lunch—just Coco and us boys. Our normal Saturday lunch: open-faced wiener sandwiches decorated with mustard smiley faces, potato chips, sweet pickles, and giant tumblers of cold milk. If we cleaned our plates, there were Fig Newtons for dessert.

Dad was rarely home on Saturdays because he spent the day tending his hospitalized patients. He said Saturdays were less hurried, so he had more time to spend with each one. He failed to add that Saturday hospital rounds were more peaceful than being at home.

Adults were always telling us kids what a wonderful dad we had and what a great doctor he was, but we had our doubts. How could he be such a great doctor if his patients were in the hospital?

Right in the middle of our lunch and a scintillating conversation about Mikey's navel and why it stuck out, Coco bolted from her chair yelling, "My onions. They're coming. I can feel it. My Vidalias are coming."

Coco sometimes got "feelings." Mostly they were feelings about people—relatives or close friends.

"Oh, my, something is going on with your Uncle Pete," she'd say in the middle of vacuuming the hall carpet. "I can feel it. Something's wrong. I'm calling Irma."

She'd drop the vacuum and call Aunt Irma, and sure enough, there was something going on with Uncle Pete—a hay fire in the barn or constipation or something of that ilk—and Aunt Irma would tell Coco all about it, over and over again. They'd be on the phone talking long distance for an hour, maybe longer, which meant that Coco was going to be running to the mailbox every day for the next month to grab the phone bill before Dad saw it and blew a gasket.

But sometimes Coco's "feelings" were about things—special things she had some sort of spiritual connection with, like her Vidalia onions.

So, as I was saying, on this particular Saturday, Coco jumped up from our lunch yelling about onions. She sprinted through the kitchen, around the corner by the phone stand, down the entrance hall, and threw open the front door, letting it bang hard against the wall behind her. Joey, Ricky, Harry, and I followed, leaving a trail of potato chips behind us. Mikey sat straitjacketed in his high chair, screaming, "My, too, Coco. My, too, Coco."

His English wasn't very good yet, but it didn't really matter. Nobody was listening.

The day was bright and warm. Robins pecked their way around our front yard hunting early-season worms. The buttercups were in full bloom. Coco stood on the front porch, using her balled-up lunch napkin to shade her eyes, craning her neck to see around the Big Curve.

"What is it, Coco? What is it? Who's coming? What are we doing?" We bobbed around her like startled chicks trying to figure out what was going on.

"Thought I heard a truck," she said, shaking her head like somebody was doing something wrong. "My Vidalias are coming. I can feel it sure as there's a God in heaven. Sure as Jesus has saved my soul. Sure as . . . [Coco had a long list of *sure ases*.] But I don't see . . ."

About that time, a white delivery van came poking around the Big Curve. Giant red letters on its side read MEL'S DELIVERY SERVICE. Underneath in blue letters it said, AIN'T NO SMELL ON MEL . . . FAST CAREFUL DEPENDABLE SERVICE.

Coco, waving her arms like the relatives were coming, bounded down the sidewalk headed for the driveway. "Here. Over here," she yelled, as if the pimple-faced delivery boy couldn't possibly have figured that out. She jumped and whooped like an Elvis fan. It was embarrassing—right out there in public like that.

It's the first time I remember thinking, *My mom might be nuts.*

Coco's onions arrived in sturdy brown boxes the size of dorm-room refrigerators. After the delivery boy lugged the boxes to the Little Den door, Coco grabbed him by the shirt collar and hung on until she'd checked her little jewels for damage. Satisfied, she sent the startled kid on his way, lecturing as he scrambled back into his van that her Vidalia onions required careful handling—a little something to remember.

It was another Coco rule: Nobody messes with my Vidalias.

Coco ooh'd and aah'd over the pink grapefruit my Aunt Wiese sent us at Christmas. They came from Texas. She ooh'd and aah'd over the tomatoes Uncle Pete delivered in August. They came from the family farm in Jackson, Tennessee. But she saved her longest ooooohs and aaaaahs for the Vidalia onions Aunt Tilde and Uncle Buck—solid Jolley relatives—sent us every spring from *over in Georgia.*

Unlike grapefruit or tomatoes, Vidalia onions were something of a prize. Back in the fifties, they were tough to come by and their scarcity supported a ladderlike hierarchy of onion privilege.

Those who lived in the small farming community of Vidalia in the Great State of Georgia sat on the top rung of the onion ladder. They took what they wanted as the prized onions came out of the field, before news of the onion harvest spread like a pandemic across the state.

Those fortunate enough to live in the Great State of Georgia and know somebody in Vidalia sat one rung down—so-called second-rungers. When second-rungers caught wind of the harvest, they overwhelmed Ma Bell with calls to Vidalia, drove the family station wagon over the next weekend, and picked up their haul in orange mesh bags or boxes.

Lucky for the rest of us Jolleys, Aunt Tilde and Uncle Buck were longtime second-rungers who drove a big station wagon.

We who lived beyond the Georgia state line but were related by blood to first- or second-rungers, clung precariously to the third rung. We got our Vidalias because we knew somebody who knew somebody who grew the celebrated onions. As a result, we relied heavily on staying in the good graces of our Georgia relatives. Without their beneficence we risked falling in among those unfortunate folks who neither lived in Georgia nor had Georgia relations. Those poor people didn't even know where to look for the ladder and almost never got their hands on Vidalias. When they did, it was only because one of us third-rungers had experienced some momentary weakness and given them one or two.

Every year our Vidalias came with a short note from Aunt Tilde, saying how delighted she was to send us some of *her* special onions. In her peachy-sweet Georgia drawl, she'd spend a few sentences reminding us that Vidalias were tough to come by. Just before a heartfelt "sincerely," she'd throw in a few words about how lucky we were to be getting them.

Aunt Tilde's note was my favorite part of our Vidalia onion tradition because it set off Dad's annual rant about damn uppity Georgia people looking down their damn noses at us Tennessee people just because some damn hick farmer grew some damn onion that tasted like every other damn onion as far as he was damn concerned. It was a deliciously predictable diatribe full of foul language.

One time Dad said we boys could use "damn" anytime we wanted if we were describing Georgia people. But Coco said "over my dead body" and "your father is forgetting his manners."

Knowing full well who buttered her onions, Coco'd sit down and write a nice note to Aunt Tilde saying how lucky we were to have such wonderful, generous Georgia relatives who favored us with some of their bounty, and how we were eternally in their debt, and oh how we wished there were some way we could repay them, but how anything we'd do to repay them couldn't possibly be as grand as sending folks Vidalia onions, and thank you thank you thank you.

It was an insurance policy she took out every year.

Coco fussed over her onions like they were newborns. She unpacked them one by one and lay them out all over the breakfast-room table. She held them up to the light, examining their skins. She used an old toothbrush to brush away lingering Georgia clay. She talked to them while she worked—cooing about pot roast made with Vidalias instead of Lipton Onion Soup Mix.

Coco saved her panty hose—just the legs—whenever a pair went bad. She kept them in a Florsheim shoe box on top of the locker freezer in the laundry room. When her Vidalias were ready for storage, she'd put her shoe box on the table next to her spiffed-up onions and sock them away, shoving an onion in a panty-hose leg and tying it off with a knot, shoving another one in and tying it off, and on and on until the leg was full of onions. She'd fill twenty or thirty panty-hose legs with six to eight onions each, and hang them from hooks sunk deep into the heavy wooden beams that ran across the ceiling of the laundry room.

From early summer through early winter, hundreds of panty-hosed onions hung there like stalactites from the ceiling of a cave. If one of us kids headed to the laundry room to retrieve a pair of socks or clean underwear, Coco somehow knew it. She hollered from wherever she was, "Nobody messes with my onions."

"Yes, ma'am," we'd yell back, and bend almost double to avoid Coco's onions on our way to the laundry basket.

Whenever Coco wanted one of her onions, she'd go into the laundry room and cut it from the bottom of a panty-hose leg, leaving the next onion up supported by the knot below it. She never trusted any of us—not even Dad—with scissors around her onions. I'm quite sure Dad didn't care. (Come to think of it, he may not have known there were panty-hosed onions hanging from the laundry-room ceiling.) But because snipping onions was forbidden, it was something we boys hungered to do.

Coco was devoted to her onion storage system. She was normally a take-things-in-stride kind of lady, but due to her abundance of red hair, she could occasionally get riled up and feisty about things other folks didn't care much about. The subject of onion storage could get under her skin. When she got somebody cornered on the subject of onion storage, she sounded a lot like her sermonizing father, Grandy Jolley.

She was not alone. Mrs. Birdsong, our neighbor a few doors down, was a panty-hose storage devotee, too, but that had not always been the case. Mrs. Birdsong had started off as an under-the-bed storage person. Like Mrs. Bradley Smith, Mrs. Mallory, and Mrs. Whitley, she'd believed in wrapping the onions individually in newspaper and storing them in single layers in flat boxes under beds all over the house.

But one year, a really bad smell began emanating from Mr. Birdsong's side of the bed, causing Mrs. Birdsong to accuse him of fouling their marital nest. Mr. Birdsong, of course, took offense and vehemently denied it, but he had to admit there was a powerful odor developing in the vicinity of his bedside table. As best he could figure it, a field rat had gotten inside the bedroom wall somewhere behind the headboard and died. As the stench got worse, Mr. Birdsong, who had a sensitive nose, moved to the sleeping porch.

It took a few days, but Mrs. Birdsong finally figured out that a box of long-forgotten onions had gone bad under the bed. She threw them out, and after consulting with Coco, who proudly showed off her system, including her shoe box and toothbrush, Mrs. Birdsong turned to panty hose.

Aunt Irma grew regular onions in her kitchen garden, but, according to her, nothing she grew could compare with Vidalias, so she got boxes from Aunt Tilde, too. In her basement, she kept a dead refrigerator where she stored nothing but Vidalia onions, saying her onions would be safe from marauding mice and nosy neighbors. Not only did she make sure those onions didn't touch one another on the refrigerator racks but every few weeks she went down to the basement and turned each and every one so the racks they sat on wouldn't bruise them and cause rotting.

Coco thought that was a little over-the-top. Standing amid her panty-hosed onions, talking on the wall phone in the laundry room, she told anybody who'd listen that Aunt Irma was something of a kook.

Annie and I now live in Walla Walla, Washington, where local farmers grow the famous Walla Walla Sweet onions.

A few weeks ago, I sent Uncle Buck and Aunt Tilde a big box of them. I attached a nice note saying how delighted we were to send them some of *our* fabulous Walla Walla Sweets, that the onions could be difficult to come by, and how lucky they were to have Walla Walla relations.

I haven't gotten a thank-you note from Aunt Tilde yet, but I'm sure it'll be arriving any day now.

11

Pee Rock

So, that was a glimpse into the old neighborhood and a look at the moms. Here's a glimpse into the first social club I joined and the early development of my social skills . . .

In the spring of '58, Possum, Junior, and Chat were eight. Lexi and I were seven. Davy Crockett was all the rage. And General Mills knew it.

We begged our moms to buy boxes of Wheaties—the big ones with the Davy Crockett special offer advertised on the front—and they did. As soon as Coco returned from the grocery store with the box, I ripped it open, stuck my hand in, and dug down to the bottom until I found a piece of paper. It turned out to be a coupon, which was a disappointment. But I dutifully sent it, along with a quarter, to someplace in Kentucky. The promise was that Davy Crockett's people

would send me an official interest in the old Davy Crockett homestead and a certificate making me an official Crockett Ranger.

A few weeks later, a box arrived in the mail. In it was a tiny burlap
bag that contained about a half cup of dirt. That was my interest in
Davy Crockett's homestead. And with the bag of dirt came a rolled-
up certificate that was nice and official-looking. It named me, Sammy
McLeod, a Crockett Ranger.

Bags of dirt and certificates in hand, Possum, Junior, Chat, Lexi,
and I formed a club. We called ourselves the Crockett Rangers of
Nashville, Tennessee. And even though Lexi was technically a girl,
she was one of us. She was a club member just like the rest of us,
mostly because she didn't cut little hearts out of pink construction
paper, could throw as well as any of us boys, and cared not one whit
for dolls or dollhouses.

Most of the time, we boys were oblivious to the fact that Lexi was
a girl. We were generally aware the doctor had cut Lexi's wiener off
when she was a baby to turn her into a girl, but none of us, including
Lexi, cared much one way or the other. If she wasn't concerned about
losing her wiener, why should we be?

We Crockett Rangers of Nashville, Tennessee, stored our club stuff
in a cigar box. It was full of important club memorabilia, including our
pop-bottle-cap collection, saved until we had enough bottle caps to get
five tickets to the Saturday-matinee picture show at the Belle Meade
Theater, where we'd see a Lone Ranger movie and eat Junior Mints.
We kept our five bags of Davy Crockett homestead dirt in that box,
too, along with our official Crockett Ranger certificates. We buried the
cigar box under a big rock just inside the entrance to the Cave.

From the Cave's entrance we had sweeping views of the entire valley. We could see neighborhood houses, farm equipment lumbering
along the Big Road below us, and bedsheets rippling in the breeze on
clotheslines in our backyards. Sunlight glinted off the surface of Moccasin Creek as it meandered its way under the canopy of ageless trees

that lined its banks. And of course we could keep tabs on intruders.

Below the Cave was a big flat rock that stuck out of the side of the hill and hung just a few feet over the hillside below it—a small ledge. It was a good lookout rock and any other club would undoubtedly have called it Lookout Rock. But we called it Pee Rock.

Now, I can't tell you exactly how our peeing contests started. Innocently enough, I'm sure.

When nature called, we boys did what boys in the woods are supposed to do: we unzipped our flies, pulled our little things out, and let fly wherever we happened to be. There was something unusually satisfying about peeing wherever we wanted, without any moms around to call us down for it. There was a lot of freedom in it.

But as we all know, freedom carries with it certain burdens and responsibilities. We learned the hard way that we shouldn't pee into the wind. And we learned that we shouldn't throw our coats on the ground next to where we were going to pee, because no matter how hard we tried, some pee always got on our coats, and even when our coats dried, we knew there were still pee germs. Your fellow Crockett Rangers would not let you in the Cave with pee germs on your coat.

Over time some club rules also came into being. For example, we agreed there would be no peeing uphill of the Cave entrance, because Possum had let loose from up there one afternoon and the wind had caught his yellow stream just right and his pee had blown right down onto the rest of us club members sitting there. And Chat had gotten some in his mouth, which caused him to fly into a rage, pin Possum to the ground, and force him to eat a leaf that had some of Possum's pee on it. Possum's unthinking pee almost tore our little club apart.

Of course, Lexi was allowed to pee anywhere she wanted, because peeing from a squat did not pose the same windblown risks. But even though she didn't have to follow the pee rules, she did anyway, saying that club members should all follow the same rules.

Well, as is true in any developing society, these basic rules took on a life of their own until most of our afternoons at the Cave were spent arguing over rules and making up more of them. Eventually, the rules became so complex and unwieldy that we finally agreed: henceforth and forever more, all club members would pee from the Pee Rock, facing downhill, and into an area known as No-Man's-Land. It was a good rule.

Boys being boys, pretty soon we were engaged in daily contests to see who could pee the farthest downhill from that rock. We used a red-painted stick to mark the location of the longest pee, and the stick stood there until the spot was surpassed by an even greater Herculean peeing effort.

Lexi, a nonparticipant in our distance-peeing contests, was a good sport and volunteered to move the marker stick anytime a new record was set. By and by, she became our contest judge, standing downhill of the contestants on the edge of No-Man's-Land, observing pee distances, and placing the red-painted stick wherever she determined it should go. According to Lexi, her decisions were final.

Distance-peeing so captured our imaginations that we boys started preparing for the competition long before it was to be held each afternoon. We gulped down water, Kool-Aid, and milk so that by the time we arrived at Pee Rock, we were chugged full of liquid. With overflowing bladders and knees knocking, we waddled onto Pee Rock while Lexi took up her spot. Then we unzipped and let fly—our distended bladders facilitating maximum pee distance.

While I cannot substantiate this claim, it is my considered opinion that, for at least the entire year 1958, we Crockett Rangers of Nashville, Tennessee, were the most accomplished urinators on the planet.

One day we arrived at the Cave, and before we could take up our positions on Pee Rock, Lexi announced that she wouldn't be judging; she planned to compete.

You can imagine the looks and our amazement. We boys knew

that without a wiener, there was no way she could participate, much less win. Chat laughed out loud. But before we could say anything, Lexi pulled off her underwear under her skirt (yes, she normally wore blue jeans but sometimes showed up in a skirt) and proceeded to climb the old sycamore tree that hung out over Pee Rock.

She climbed at least twenty feet before she stopped. She turned to face downhill with her back against the tree. She put one foot on a branch that shot off to the left and her other foot on a branch that shot off to the right, and squatted down, straddling the gap between those branches. Hiking up her skirt, she licked her finger and held it up in the air, waiting for a strong following wind. When the wind came up, Lexi let fly a stream of pee the likes of which you've never seen. It splattered well beyond the previous record held by one of us boys. It was a peeing effort for the ages.

And then, lickety-split, Lexi flew out of that tree and ran downhill to find the farthest point of pee moisture. She made a mark on the ground with the heel of her tennis shoe and then scampered partway back uphill to grab the red marker, which she carried back downhill and stuck in the ground at the site of her new record.

We boys stood by the Cave entrance gawking as Lexi came strutting back uphill. She stood there in front of us with her balled-up fists on her hips and a faint smile on her lips. We could all tell a storm of protest was about to erupt, about breaking the rules and so on and so forth. You could just feel it in the air.

But surprisingly, not one of us boys said a word. Even at that age, we admired creativity and determination. And Lexi had just exhibited a heap of both. We just nodded our heads and smiled. Lexi nodded and smiled back.

And then we went on to other important club business.

Now, that would be a pretty good place to end this tale, with a little moral about women competing in a man's world, or the integration of men's clubs and breaking into the old boys' network, or how much more intelligent and creative women are than men when they put their minds to it. And all the female readers of this story could nod their heads in agreement and smile at the wisdom.

But here's how it really ended:

Next day when we boys arrived at the Cave, Lexi was there ahead of us. She'd moved the official marker back uphill to its previous world-record spot, a record set by one of us boys.

She said she'd thought about it overnight and realized there could be some argument about the legitimacy of her record. She wasn't too worried about that, she said, because she was the official judge and her decisions were final. But what did concern her was the simple fact that none of us boys would ever develop the bladder strength necessary to beat her record. Which meant her record would put an end to our contests, an era in our club's history would pass, and the championship peeing tradition we'd developed would die a sudden death.

She didn't want her record to end our game, so she was withdrawing it and going back to being the judge, because we were a club and tradition was important. That game was a part of what we Crockett Rangers were all about.

12

On the Road
Missoula, Montana

I left the farm and headed for Missoula, Montana—first stop on the road to enlightenment.

Annie opened the gate for me. She handed me a thermos of coffee, a brown paper sack full of Honey Crisp apples, and a half-eaten box of whole-wheat crackers that tasted like dirt.

"No salt and loaded with fiber," she said, pecking me on the cheek. "Summer's fixing you a special dinner tonight, so don't ruin your appetite on roadside junk food. Now get along, Sam, and try to have some fun."

■　■　■

Annie and I have three daughters. I grew up among boys but fathered a houseful of girls. As you might imagine, I made the transition from boys to girls with some difficulty.

Annie says that's an understatement.

Summer, our oldest, lives in Missoula with her husband, Rusty, who's finishing up a degree in forestry at the University of Montana and then getting a job, I hope. While Rusty studies, Summer teaches high school English, coaches a girls' soccer team, and chitchats with her mom and sisters on subjects they avoid around me—mostly novel ways to spend money and analysis of the men in their lives. (I regularly get evaluated and generally come up short.)

I pulled up in front of their house at dusk. The tiny, two-bedroom, wood-sided bungalow sat on a postage-stamp-size lot. The porch light burned brightly above a small wicker table and two chairs. A dog leash hung from a hook by the front door.

Summer, an enthusiastic participant in life, was on the lookout for me. Blonde ponytail bobbing behind her, blue eyes sparkling, pot holder in hand, she sprinted to the car and jumped into my arms. Rusty, a tall, dark-haired, triathlete-kind-of-guy, was close behind her, collaring their equally enthusiastic wolf-size dog, Haley.

After a short tour of home improvements and a demonstration of Haley's new tricks (including "lie down," my favorite), Summer pulled a casserole of her heart-stopping macaroni and cheese from the oven and set it on a trivet. A pot of vegetable soup simmered on the stovetop. The smells wafted over me and my knees went weak. The Jolley gene moved to a heightened state of alert.

I uncorked the Walla Walla wine Annie sent with me and we ate while the kids caught me up on Rusty's thesis topic (something to do with religion and global warming; can't say that I understood it, but it sounded scholarly), Summer's soccer team (they've got a shot at the state title), and the difficulties of finding day care for a dog that looks like she could eat you (and might try).

"So, enough about us," Summer spouted. "We want to hear about your old girlfriend. Mom says you're driving all the way to Nashville to visit an old flame."

"She wasn't my girlfriend," I said, a little exasperated.

"That's not what Coco told Mom. Coco said you and Lexi were inseparable. She said Lexi was your first love."

"Well, sorry to poke a hole in your balloon, but she wasn't." I took another bite of macaroni and cheese. "Lexi was just one of the kids in the neighborhood where I grew up. We're having a reunion of sorts— or at least, that's what I'm guessing it is—and your mother pushed me to go. Can't say I'm all that excited about it. Look at this gray beard. And this belly. I'm too old for this foolishness."

Summer shook her head. "Nobody's gonna care what you look like, Dad. They're too busy worrying about their own looks. And if she wasn't your girlfriend, why are you fretting about looking good? Wonder what *she* looks like now? You're taking a camera, aren't you? I can't wait to see pictures. You haven't told Jolie and Marshall, have you? Has Mom called them? This is so cool! My very own dad is going to visit an old girlfriend! I thought this stuff only happened in movies. I'm calling them."

Summer jumped up from the table, grabbed her cell phone, and sprinted to the front porch to call her sisters, letting the screen door slam behind her.

"Your ladies are on it," Rusty quipped.

"Yep, and not paying a bit of attention to anything I say, are they?"

"Nope," Rusty said. "Want a piece of carrot cake? Summer made it for you. Pretty good."

"Sure," I said. "But just a sliver. I ate more macaroni and cheese than I should have. I'm trying to lose a few pounds."

"Right," Rusty said.

13

The Day Before the Big Day

Summer's macaroni and cheese reminds me of Christmas Eve. We McLeods ate macaroni and cheese, alongside our turkey, dressing, sweet potatoes, cheesy asparagus casserole, raspberry Jell-O salad, and dinner rolls. And it wasn't ordinary macaroni and cheese, either . . .

Christmas Eve was the same every year. About noon, Granddaddy McLeod wheeled his Oldsmobile 98 into the driveway and honked the horn like the light had turned green and the idiot in front of him was checking his teeth in the rearview mirror instead of watching the road.

Once his big boat was docked, Granddaddy helped my grandmother Mimi from the front seat, not because she couldn't get out of the car on her own but because she was so deep in casseroles wrapped in old blankets that she couldn't see to move without tipping her raspberry Jell-O salad into the driveway.

Dad helped Aunt Wiese, his older sister, out of the backseat. She had a coconut cake in a tin on her lap and boiled custard in a quart jar on the seat beside her. Her feet were buried under nicely wrapped presents—lots of them.

We called her "Wiese" because, when I was a youngster, I couldn't say "Louise" very well. The name stuck.

I was told that she'd moved in with my grandparents after her husband was killed in the Korean War and had lived with them ever since. As far as I know, she never worked or went out with other men. She was Mimi's constant companion. She traveled with my grandparents whenever they came to visit.

Wiese was a good-looking woman. If anybody in the McLeod family had a claim on the word *glamorous* it was Aunt Wiese. Her blue eyes shimmered behind silver frames decorated with pink diamonds. She wore velvet hats with plastic fruit and paper flowers on them. She got her red hair from a bottle, her eyelashes off the shelf, and was no stranger to makeup. From the neck up, she was right off the pages of *Vogue*. From the neck down, she was *Cosmopolitan* without the cleavage—long, fancy dresses and tasteful high heels.

Wiese took after Granddaddy McLeod, a smooth-talking, fast-walking real estate developer who loved touring the country in his baby-blue Oldsmobile. He favored houndstooth suits, pin-striped shirts, two-tone shoes, stylish straw hats in summer, and brown felt hats in winter. And every tie was a conversation piece: we gawked at the naked angels who stood knee-deep in a river that ran from the heavens at Granddaddy's high-collared neck all the way to his silver horseshoe belt buckle.

You'd never have mistaken Granddaddy McLeod for a God-fearing, fire-and-brimstone Baptist, but he was—most of the time—and occasionally got defensive about it. "God doesn't put up with a lot of foolishness," he'd bark. "But He doesn't mind a fella lookin' good." And, "If God wanted angels in brassieres, He'd a put 'em on 'em Himself."

Mimi seemed out of place around Granddaddy and Wiese, like a blackbird living with cockatoos. Mimi wore basic black in public and an apron at home. She was a short, compact little woman sporting silver-blue hair and half-glasses you'd never have noticed had they not been attached to her bosom by a string of jewels. She traveled with a Crisco-spattered copy of *The Joy of Cooking* and was generally suspicious of anything bordering on fun.

We boys weren't much on hugging, handshaking, and lipstick kisses. We greeted our McLeod relatives just enough to get to the presents—the ones in the backseat and more stowed in the Oldsmobile's gigantic trunk. When Mimi and Wiese were safely out of the car and out of the way, we hauled the loot into our living room, divided the packages, counted them, admired them, shook them unmercifully, and tried to see through the wrappings before stacking them in neatly separated piles under the Christmas tree.

Coco didn't think much of our claiming individual territories under the tree; she viewed hoarding as evidence of greed, which it was.

While Coco showed Granddaddy and Mimi to the guest room, Dad headed for the den, where he turned on the television to warm up the tube for the Big Game. We kids toted Wiese's winter coats, suitcases, cosmetic cases, hatboxes, and shoe boxes to the Little Den—a pine-paneled room not much bigger than a walk-in closet. During the Christmas holidays, Wiese slept there on the foldout sofa in front of a fire that blazed away in the fireplace. It was a cozy retreat. And by the time we had unloaded her luggage from the Oldsmobile, the Little Den was piled high with Wiese's belongings, smelling of Chanel No. 5 and rose-scented powders.

While Wiese unpacked we went hunting. No guns. No dogs. Just inquiring minds. We opened her hatboxes and unzipped her hanging bags. There were dead animals everywhere—otter, mink, fox, ermine, and rabbit. One fox fur hat was particularly intriguing. The fox's head hung just off the edge of the hat about two inches from his tail. We stared at that fox and asked Wiese whether he'd ever catch his tail.

"Not if I can help it," she said. "If that ol' fox goes to chasing his tail, you boys whack him with somethin' hard enough to put him back to sleep. I don't like animals crawling 'round on my head."

Dad and Granddaddy parked themselves for the afternoon in front of the television to watch football games. Granddaddy unbuttoned his collar, loosened his tie so the river full of naked angels ran down his pants' leg, kicked off his fancy shoes, and commenced swearing at the TV. Periodically, he'd bounce off the sofa and kneel in front of the tube begging our merciful Lord to help the *#@%^* idiot kick the *#@%* field goal. Between outbursts, Dad would say, "Hey, Pop, let's watch the language." And we'd rack our brains trying to remember exactly what Granddaddy had yelled, knowing that there was some foul language in there somewhere.

It didn't help that between Jackson and Nashville, Granddaddy McLeod crossed an imaginary line that separated alcohol's evils from its delectations. In Jackson, he was a model of teetotaling Baptist restraint, never drinking anything stronger than a large glass of buttermilk. But in Nashville, he fell off the wagon hard enough to kill a normal man. Imbibin' was apparently essential to getting through a McLeod Christmas. During the afternoon, Granddaddy drank Pabst Blue Ribbon beer, but at five o'clock he switched over to J&B Rare Scotch, which must not have been all that rare because we always seemed to have a half-gallon of the stuff in the cupboard. By dinnertime, Granddaddy was three sheets to the wind, headed for four.

Coco, Wiese, and Mimi spent the afternoon in the kitchen preparing dinner. Except for Mimi's raspberry Jell-O salad and Wiese's coconut cake and boiled custard, Christmas Eve dinner was indistinguishable from Thanksgiving dinner: turkey, dressing, cheesy asparagus casserole, Wiese's dinner rolls, a relish tray loaded down with homemade chowchow and sweet pickles, and two macaroni-and-cheese casseroles (one with oysters and one without).

As far as I know, we McLeods were the only citizens of These United States to experiment with oysters in a macaroni-and-cheese casserole. Every time I mention this in polite company, faces contort into doubtful frowns. All I can say is, don't knock it if you haven't tried it. Of course, the unadventurous among you can make the casserole without the oysters. That's pretty good, too.

Coco's Macaroni and Cheese and Oysters

Serves 8

Ingredients

1 pound macaroni

4 cups milk

1 bay leaf

8 tablespoons (1 stick) unsalted butter

½ cup flour

1 tablespoon kosher salt

½ teaspoon freshly ground pepper

¼ teaspoon freshly grated nutmeg

4 cups sharp Cheddar cheese (grated)

1 teaspoon Worcestershire sauce

1 quart medium, plump, fresh-shucked oysters (well drained)

PREHEAT oven to 400°.

COOK the macaroni according to the directions on the package, salting the cooking water with one teaspoon of the kosher salt. Drain the macaroni and set it aside.

IN a medium saucepan, heat the milk and bay leaf until the milk is hot, but not boiling. Remove the bay leaf.

IN a large Dutch oven or pot, melt the butter over medium heat. Whisk in the flour and continue to cook over medium heat for two minutes. Add the hot milk slowly, whisking until the sauce comes to a slow simmer and thickens. Remove the sauce from the heat, add the remaining salt, pepper, nutmeg, cheese, and Worcestershire sauce, and stir to combine. Then fold in the cooked macaroni.

SPOON the macaroni and cheese into a deep-sided nine-by-twelve-inch casserole dish and place it in the oven uncovered. Bake for thirty to forty minutes, just until the macaroni and cheese is heated through, lightly browned, and bubbling. Remove the casserole from the oven, add the oysters, stir to combine, and return the casserole to the oven. Bake an additional five minutes or so, until the oysters are hot but not overcooked.

YOU'RE going to like this better than you think!

Coco and Wiese took an occasional drink but never drank around Mimi. Mimi took her religion seriously and openly disapproved of Pabst Blue Ribbon beer. She said they should pour it back into the horse.

But there came a year when Mimi, our tiny gray-haired grandma, said in her whisper of a voice that she'd like to try "a whiskey drink." Coco grabbed the icebox handle to keep from falling down. Wiese picked her lower jaw up off the floor. There was a moment of silence. And then Coco hauled Mimi into her arms and danced around the kitchen. Mimi was stepping out.

Sipping one of Coco's famous whiskey sours, Mimi progressed from prim to party girl. While Coco toiled over the turkey and dressing and Wiese mixed up her cheesy asparagus casserole, Mimi sat legs akimbo on the kitchen floor with us and played tiddledywinks, sometimes sending a wink into a casserole, cackling like a schoolgirl, and ordering a top-up on her whiskey sour (which she never got).

By six-thirty, dinner was ready. The adults crowded around the dining-room table. We boys sat at a card table in the living room, where we could wrinkle up our noses at the thought of oysters in macaroni and cheese without getting a lecture. "If you don't have anything good to say about the food, don't say anything at all," Coco'd preach. And while there was nothing in that lecture about turned-up noses, unpleasant facial expressions were, according to Coco, also prohibited.

The grown-ups lingered over dinner as if they were enjoying it, even though we could tell they mostly weren't. After a proper Baptist blessing delivered by Granddaddy, he started his annual Christmas Eve speech about all the ways Baptists were better than Methodists and how disappointed he was that we boys weren't being raised right. "Casual Christians," he called us, and took another sip of his J&B Rare Scotch.

And every year, Coco tried a little peacemaking, explaining for the umpteenth time that her father, Grandy Jolley, was a Methodist minister and we were being raised Methodist out of respect for his vocation. We Nashville McLeods had nothing against Baptists, but we were sticking with the Methodists.

Unfortunately, Coco's offer of the olive branch did nothing but spur Granddaddy into a J&B Rare Scotch–inspired Baptist rage.

The annual battle between Baptists and Methodists ended when Coco, her red hair flashing like the light on a fire truck, spanked the table loud enough to shut Granddaddy down and said she'd reconsider her position if Granddaddy became a Baptist minister, but not before. With that, she stood up, saying it was time for dessert, and went to hide the bottle of scotch. It was the McLeod version of an interfaith war.

Wiese's coconut cake and boiled custard topped off our Christmas Eve dinner and led the way to grudging reconciliation between

Granddaddy McLeod and Coco. We kids loved the custard, mostly because it came with Reddi-wip and a cherry on top. But we were skeptical of the cake. We thought it tasted better if you scraped the coconut from the icing and piled it on the edge of your plate. Coco warned us that she'd rip our tongues from our heads if we told Wiese how we felt about coconut. "You boys are gonna smile and tell Wiese how much you love her cake. It's Wiese's favorite—she's proud of that cake—and you boys are not going to ruin Wiese's Christmas. Got it?" We held on to our tongues and nodded. We got it.

After dessert, Dad went off to the bathroom. Shortly after he left, we heard sleigh bells coming from somewhere outside the house. We ran to the front door. Coco opened it and headed into the front yard to look up on the roof. There was nothing up there, but she found bits of carrot scattered on the lawn, evidence that reindeer had tromped around in the yard long enough to have a snack before heading on to a house where the good little children were tucked away, sleeping soundly in their beds.

That was enough to send us scrambling for our pajamas. Meanwhile, Wiese found our Christmas book in her suitcase.

Every Christmas, Wiese brought us a new book, usually a chapter book that had enough pictures in it to keep our attention. By the time we arrived in the Little Den, ready for reading time, Wiese had placed four tasseled bookmarks in the book, dividing it into four equal parts so we'd read about the same number of words each night and finish on her last night in Nashville.

Coco stoked the fire while Wiese turned out all the lights except her reading lamp. We climbed up next to the foldout sofa and settled in under the blankets that Coco had stacked there for Wiese's comfort. Coco went back to the kitchen to clean up the dishes while Wiese read to us.

She had a beautiful lilt to her reading voice—a soft rising and falling that held our interest but rocked us to sleep. Firelight danced on the walls. Big oak logs crackled and sputtered as they burned. Sparks rose on hot air up the chimney while Wiese read, stopping every so often to show us the pictures.

And then it was Christmas morning . . .

14

Getting Some Religion

We got a dose of Baptist religion during the Christmas holiday from Granddaddy McLeod, but Reverend Ben served up our regular, weekly religion at Belle Meade Methodist Church. We McLeods were there every Sunday in front-row seats . . .

Coco may not have gotten us manners, but that failure did nothing to slow her efforts to get us some religion. Like it or not, we were Methodized every week.

Belle Meade Methodist Church, a tiny yellow-brick box with a copper-sided steeple, sat on a lonely corner surrounded by sapling maples, right next to a pitch-and-putt golf course and driving range.

We casual but otherwise good Christians went to church on Sundays while what Mrs. Bradley Smith called "golf-happy heathens" (her husband being a prime example) went to the driving range and whacked red-striped, driving-range golf balls into the church parking lot, occasionally bouncing one harmlessly off the stained-glass windows that ran the length of the church sanctuary. Flexible glass, I guess.

We McLeods sat in the Toad waiting for a break in the barrage, then bolted from our car and sprinted across the parking lot and up the sanctuary steps to safety in God's loving embrace. It was a Sunday-morning test of faith—as close as we got to the Valley of the Shadow of Death. And while we feared no evil, the heathens did not yell "fore" like they were supposed to, so there was plenty of danger in the air, and we loved it.

You could never tell when one of us casual Christians might get bonked on the head and, if all went well, die. Unfortunately, we never witnessed a direct hit. But we did see Mrs. Bradley Smith duck and cover one day when Possum snuck up behind his mom and yelled "fore" in her ear. Possum liked to play jokes on folks—particularly his mom.

Mrs. Bradley Smith dove to the pavement, hit her head so hard she got a bloody gash, and badly twisted an ankle. She lay on her back, huffing and puffing, fanning herself with her pocket Bible, yelling at Possum to stand still because she was planning to murder him when she got back on her feet, and ordering Junior to get her Benson & Hedges off the front seat of the car. While Junior retrieved the Superslims, my dad, who was a doctor (but not the kind that stitched people back together), examined Mrs. Bradley Smith's cranium, handed her his handkerchief to stanch the bleeding, said she'd probably live (a minor disappointment to us kids), and suggested a trip to the emergency room and a call to Dr. Pritchard just in case.

While Coco ran into the church to call the good Dr. Pritchard, Dad, with our help, hoisted Mrs. Bradley Smith onto her good leg and prodded her toward the Toad, where she leaned against the car door, a Superslim bobbing between her lips, yelling profanities at the heathens and shaking her fist at God.

We'd never seen an injured mom and were surprised at all the moaning and foul language. Granddaddy McLeod used dirty words all the time, but nobody else in our little universe did. We didn't know that Mrs. Bradley Smith even knew those words, much less used them. Most were directed at the golf-happy heathens, but God and Possum came in for their fair share.

If God was ever going to smite a person for foul language, this was the time. But it didn't happen. There were no lightning bolts or floods or anything. Apparently the use of foul language was not as risky as moms made it out to be.

Sunday school at Belle Meade Methodist Church was taught by well-intentioned congregants who didn't know any more than we kids about the Bible or the rules of Methodist living. As a consequence, we did a lot of stuff with safety scissors, glue, and colored construction paper. We mostly made daisy chains to represent the bonds placed on Hebrews or Romans or Pharisees or whoever it was that was being chained up. (I could never keep it all straight.)

At Christmas, we made cardboard cradles for the baby Jesus even though we didn't have any babies to put in them. That was just as well. Our cradles never came out right; they mostly listed one way or the other and fell over.

For Mother's Day, we made little booklets of colored paper with pictures from magazines pasted on the pages. One year I got a *Good Housekeeping*, came up with a bathroom theme, and filled my booklet with pictures of sinks, bathtubs, and toilets—all a lot fancier than the ones we McLeods had at home. Mr. Taylor, my Sunday school teacher at the time, didn't think much of the work, but Coco liked it so much she magnetized it to the refrigerator door. She said it was the nicest, most thoughtful bathroom book she'd ever received.

After we finished our paste-and-cardboard project each week, we sang "Jesus Loves Me," passed the graham crackers, and downed Hi-C fruit punch from miniature Dixie cups. That was my favorite part of being a Methodist. I loved Hi-C fruit punch. I still do.

Sunday school was followed by Big Church, where we McLeods sat in the front pew right below the pulpit. Remembering her own mother's tactics, Coco figured that: (1) the closer we were to the minister and the choir, the closer we were to God; and (2) it made sense to sit where we couldn't kick the pew in front of us and annoy folks; and (3) when we went up to the kneeling benches on Communion Sunday to get a cracker and some grape juice, the less time we spent punching each other on our way to and from the kneeling bench, the better.

Reverend Ben was a nice man in spite of being our pastor. His sermons were good stories—the lessons were well hidden, if they were there at all—and he didn't drone on too long. There was often some good pillaging in them. And the good guys always won with God's help.

We sang the same songs over and over—generally just the first and last verses. Occasionally we'd start singing an old familiar hymn and Reverend Ben would get too much into the spirit of things and throw us a curveball: he'd override the church program, saying we were going to sing all four verses for a change so we could enjoy those normally neglected middle two. Certain occupants of the McLeod pew groaned so loud that Coco had to flash her wait-till-I-get-you-home look to calm things down.

Reverend Ben's prayers, while too long, were a lot shorter than Grandy Jolley's. He let you know when he was coming to the end, because he always asked God to bless These United States and give our president some wisdom.

After Big Church, we ran past Reverend Ben, the ushers, and dawdling congregants out onto the church lawn and around the corner to the side entrance of Fellowship Hall, where church ladies were serving cookies and punch.

Fellowship Hall cookies were homemade and a big step up from graham crackers most of the time. But sometimes old Mrs. Walker made coconut macaroons. It didn't happen often, but enough that we were on guard entering Fellowship Hall. It wasn't worth suffering the old-lady-pinching-of-cheeks if the cookie trays were piled high with offerings so thoroughly laced with coconut that we couldn't pick it out. We'd rather have eaten dirt.

Fellowship Hall punch was a disappointment, mostly because the church ladies put a big can of pineapple juice and a giant bottle of ginger ale in with the Hi-C. The ginger ale was fine, but the pineapple juice tasted like the can it came in. We drank it but suggested to those ladies that Hi-C fruit punch was better by itself. If God had meant for folks to add pineapple juice, He'd have gotten them to do it at the Hi-C factory. After a full morning of getting some religion, we could get a might preachy ourselves.

Whenever we visited our McLeod relatives in Jackson, Granddaddy McLeod quizzed us unmercifully about our Methodist upbringing. And then he'd shake his head while pulling on his ears, and bellow something at Mimi or Wiese like, "I told you. Those damned Methodists are lazy. Damned casual Christians, I'm telling you. It ain't right. These boys are gettin' heads full of watered-down Methodist mush and I can't do a goddamned thing about it." And then he'd think about it for a minute, herd us into his Oldsmobile 98, and run us down to his church for some quick-fix Baptizing.

While we boys could get a little down-in-the-mouth about Methodizing, one trip to Granddaddy McLeod's Baptist church in downtown Jackson was enough to quash our complaining. The Baptist preacher could drone on like he meant it. Sundays at the Baptist church made us long for Reverend Ben and graham crackers (which were not served at the Baptist church during Sunday school on account of the fact that we were sinners and couldn't eat until we'd been prayed over sufficiently in Big Church).

As a young child, I preferred casual Methodism to the strictures of Baptism. The Baptists dunked when a sprinkle would do. Methodists enjoyed a good story, while Baptists preferred sermons that scared us witless. And Baptists could overdo praying better than the best of the Methodists. Baptists overdid most everything, and that struck me as a bad thing—until it came to food. Overdoing food seemed to me a good thing and almost worth a trip to the Baptist church. Baptist churchgoers were such overachievers that they overdid food every Sunday, but not until church services were over and we'd all been cleansed of our sins.

Instead of punch and cookies, the church ladies served up a fortifying lunch after services. Fried chicken, honey-baked ham, and homemade rolls showed up every Sunday. There were deviled eggs, celery sticks smeared with pimento cheese, potato chips and onion dip, Fritos and chili dip, squash casserole, green bean casserole, red Jell-O salad, lime-green Jell-O salad with marshmallows, Mandarin-orange Jell-O salad, chicken salad, slices of white bread, potato salad, cold green-pea salad, a big tray of sweet gherkins and pickled okra, corn relish in a Ball jar, homemade chocolate chip cookies, and all manner of homemade pies and cakes—chess pie being my favorite.

After the praying was over, the Baptist church was a good place to be. The food damned near made up for gettin' some religion.

15

Parthenon

Sometimes we went to the Parthenon after Big Church . . . really . . .

The Parthenon was built in Nashville, Tennessee, in the early 1900s as a temple honoring the goddess Athena. She was the kind of woman who preferred to talk things out and settle arguments peaceably, but if you didn't come around to her way of thinking, she'd lop your head off with a sword. In a fight, she was a goddess you wanted on your side.

I told Coco all about Athena one afternoon—right after a school field trip to the Parthenon.

"She was also a vagina," I said.

Coco looked at me funny, then stopped and thought for a second.

"Virgin," Coco said, "I think you mean 'virgin' . . . not . . ."

She never finished the sentence because she was laughing so hard she couldn't catch her breath. She couldn't even stand up. She had to sit down on the kitchen floor. Then she lay down. We boys watched her roll around the floor in the middle of the kitchen, holding her stomach. She laughed so hard we laughed, too.

We had no idea what we were laughing about, but we laughed. It was a good time.

When Coco finally got back on her feet, she held on to the edge of the stove for a long time and said, "Oh my goodness . . . oh my goodness . . . oh my goodness," before her eyes stopped watering.

"So, what's a virgin?" Ricky asked.

Coco started to say something, almost started laughing again, but caught herself and said instead, "How would you boys like something to eat?"

"Yea!" we yelled.

We were easily distracted.

The Parthenon sits in the middle of Centennial Park, which is full of giant oak trees, expansive lawns, well-manicured gardens, duck ponds, and a lot of stuff painted city-park green—old-time swing sets, monkey bars, park benches, and solid wooden picnic tables under wood-beamed open-air pavilions.

During the fall, when it was too cold to go swimming but too nice outside to go roller-skating at the Hippodrome, Coco took us to Centennial Park to play and feed the ducks. The park was pretty close to Cross Keys Restaurant where we went on Sundays to get our manners.

"Lemme have some," Joey demanded. "I wanna feed the ducks, too."

"Me, too," Ricky said.

"Me, too," Harry echoed.

"Okay, okay," I said. "Hold your horses."

In Coco's absence, I was in charge and got to say things like "hold your horses," which is what she'd have said had she been there. I also got to dole out partially frozen bread crusts from a plastic bag the size of a grocery sack—one of the great privileges of age.

I was in charge because Coco was still getting Mikey out of his car seat. It was made of rusty steel and had a toy steering wheel with a squeaky horn that Coco had disabled with a screwdriver so it wouldn't make *that noise*. The seat hung on the back of the Toad's front seat next to Coco. In a front-end collision, it would have launched Mikey right through the windshield, taking the rearview mirror with him as he sailed by.

After years of abuse, the car seat's flimsy restraining belt had finally disintegrated, so Coco had replaced it with a rope, which meant she had to tie Mikey into his seat with a knot that never wanted to come loose. Coco spent a goodly portion of her thirties fiddling with knots.

For the next hour we fed the Centennial Park ducks—obese, lily-white, blimplike fowl with orange beaks and orange webbed feet. They waddled around us trying to peck holes in our plastic bread bag or snatch bread trimmings from our hands before we could throw them into the pond, where there was too much competition from goldfish—little fellows released from aquariums all over Nashville that fed on nutritious white bread and grew as big and ugly as Charlie the Tuna.

Invariably a duck tried to take one of our fingers off, causing us to retreat to the safety of the car. While hundreds of ducks milled about on the ground outside, Coco examined the damaged appendage, painted it with Mercurochrome, bandaged it, pronounced it good as new, and sent us back to the pond, where the feeding frenzy resumed.

"Why are these ducks white?" Ricky wanted to know. "The ones at the farm are brown," he added.

"All these ducks ever eat is white bread," Coco said. "You'd be white as a sheet, too, if all you ate was white bread."

That made as much sense as anything else.

■   ■   ■

"What's that thing?" Harry wanted to know, pointing at the Parthenon.

"The Parthenon, silly," Coco replied.

"Where'd it come from?" Harry asked.

"It's always been there," Coco said. She now had a curious look on her face.

"Never seen *that* before," Harry said.

Coco looked alarmed. We fed the ducks in the shadow of the Parthenon all the time. Next to the L&C Tower downtown, the Parthenon was the biggest thing we'd ever seen. Somehow Harry had missed it.

"Does anybody live there?" Harry asked.

"No," Coco said.

"What do they sell there?"

"Nothing," Coco said.

"Do people eat in there?"

"No," Coco said, looking seriously concerned. Harry seemed to be suffering from some sort of early-onset dementia.

"Well, what good is it?" Harry asked.

"It's not good for anything," Joey said. "It's just the Parthenon, okay? Stop asking so many damn questions and hand over the bread."

Coco whacked Joey with her pocketbook.

"Ow," Joey said.

"Watch your mouth," Coco said, and marched toward the Toad. "C'mon, boys."

It was getting dark.

"Can we swing, Coco?" Ricky asked.

"No," Coco said, still marching toward the car.

"Just five minutes?"

"No."

Coco picked Mikey up so we could move a little faster.

"Just two minutes."

"No."

"Just one minute."

Coco turned on Ricky, "No. N . . . O . . . NO."

Ricky started to cry. Joey bopped Harry. Harry started to cry. Coco told Joey to leave Harry alone or she'd bop him. Harry's crying set Mikey off. Joey said I was too chicken to bop him. So I bopped him. Joey started crying. Coco bopped me with her purse and said it was time for some food.

"Life will be better when we get something to eat," Coco said, sounding more hopeful than convinced. "Your dad's going to a meeting and won't be home for dinner, so let's go to the Krystal and get dinner before I have myself committed to a mental institution."

"Yea!" we yelled.

During the fall, Dad rarely came home for dinner. It was flu season. He had lots of heart patients in the hospital, and he made house calls nearly every night, often in the middle of the night. When he wasn't tending the infirm, he was going to medical meetings. It was like tax season for accountants, only worse.

If Dad wasn't coming home, Coco took us out for dinner. Our favorite place was the Krystal, just a hop, skip, and a jump from Centennial Park. We almost always went to the Krystal after we fed the ducks.

The Krystal was a fifties-style drive-in joint that specialized in tiny burgers, fries, and milk shakes. It was a place where we didn't have to get out of the car. Coco could dock the Toad under a long metal awning, roll down her window, reach out and pull a silver metal box off a stand, and hook it on the car door. The box had a red push button on it. She'd push the red button and pretty soon a lady would say, "Can I take your order, please?"

Coco'd push the red button and say, "Yes, please."

Everybody was nice and polite in the fifties.

After a short wait, the lady in the box would say, "Ma'am, could you speak up, please? I'm having a hard time hearing you."

That could have been because Mikey was spinning the steering wheel on his car seat as fast as it would go, bouncing up and down, and hollering "honk honk." Or it could have been because Harry was thumping Mikey in the back of the head saying, "Does that hurt?" *Thump.* "Does this hurt?" *Thump.* "Tell me when it hurts." *Thump.* Or it might have had something to do with Joey and me playing Rock Scissors Paper, slapping each other silly.

"Can I take your order, please?" the lady in the box yelled.

"We'll have twenty-five Krystal burgers—"

"Coco . . ." Harry whined.

"Just a minute, son. I'm trying to order—"

"I know," Harry said, "but, Coco . . ."

The lady in the box yelled, "Ma'am, are you still there?"

"YES," Coco yelled. "We'll have twenty-five Krystal burgers and—"

"Coco!" Harry said again.

"HARRY, I'm trying to order supper. Just hold your horses."

Coco got to say that because she was back in charge.

"We'll have twenty-five Krystal burgers, ten orders of fries—"

"But, Coco," Harry started.

"NOT NOW, HARRY, I'M TRYING TO ORDER SUPPER," Coco shrieked. She was losing it.

The lady in the box asked, "Are you okay, ma'am?"

"YES . . . I'm fine," Coco said, bringing the volume down. "We'd like twenty-five Krystal burgers . . ."

She shot Harry a mean look in the rearview mirror, defying him to interrupt her.

"And ten orders of fries and five orange sodas—small ones."

"Is that all, ma'am."

"Yes, please," Coco said, back under control and polite again.

Then Coco turned in her seat, grabbed Mikey's tiny hand so he wouldn't hit her in the eye, and said, "Okay, Harry, what was so important?"

Harry was sulking now. "Nothing," he said. "Nobody ever listens to me anyway."

"Poor little baby," Joey taunted.

"I'm sorry, son, but I was trying to order supper. What were you trying to say?" Coco repeated.

"Well, I was just wondering . . ."

"Wondering what?" Coco asked.

"Well, I was just going to ask if you know where Ricky is?"

Coco looked to her right at Mikey, then back at us. You could tell she was counting. Then she looked toward the cargo area of the Toad—what we called the Way Back. And back at us. And then at Mikey, and then she hollered, "GOD IN HEAVEN, WE'VE LOST RICKY."

Coco jammed the Toad into reverse and hit the accelerator. The metal box with the red push button attached to the Toad popped off its cord and fell into Coco's lap. While she backed, turning the steering wheel with her left hand, she tossed the metal box into the backseat with us.

Coco pointed the nose of the Toad toward West End Avenue, shifted into drive, and hit the accelerator. Tires squealed. The smell of burning rubber filled the Toad. Coco took a turn onto West End Avenue—right into rush-hour traffic—yelling as we went, "HOLD ON, BOYS."

Driving half on the street and half on the sidewalk, dodging the "No Parking" signs, Coco set a land-speed record for the Toad, skirting the stop-and-go traffic on West End as she went.

Joey yelled, "You think Ricky's still at the park, Coco?"

We were sliding all over the backseat and each other, but it wasn't as bad as it could have been. There were only three of us back there.

"Maybe somebody's snatched him!" Harry yelled. "Maybe he's been kidnapped . . ."

"Shut up," I said to Harry.

Coco was starting to cry.

A police car was behind us now—right on the Toad's tail. Its siren was blaring and the red light on top made the inside of the Toad look like the *Shock Theater* dungeon Frankenstein lived in.

"There's a policeman behind us," Harry yelled, as if we didn't already know that. Harry was on his knees on the backseat looking out the rear window.

"He looks mean, Coco. You think he's gonna start shooting at us?"

"Shut up," I said to Harry.

When we arrived at the entrance to Centennial Park, Coco took a hard right, swerved between the stone pillars with the Toad fishtailing, flew up the main drag, and wheeled around the western end of the Parthenon. She coaxed the Toad over the curb by the duck ponds and drove about fifty yards on newly mowed grass toward the playground. The Toad's headlights jumped all over the place but settled down when Coco hit the brakes and pointed the car at the swing sets.

There sat Ricky, on the ground under the seat of a swing, crying his eyes out. Coco jumped out of the Toad, ran to the swings, grabbed him, and hugged him like she'd never hugged anybody before. She was crying harder than Ricky.

It took a while for Coco to calm down and explain things to the policeman. He wasn't mean. He was nice—a little confused maybe, but nice.

He took Coco's name and insurance information, saying she'd probably have to pay something for the damage to the grass. But after that, he helped her back into the car. We piled into the backseat.

Ricky was with us this time, but just to make sure, Coco counted heads before backing the Toad off the park lawn.

"Are we going back to get our Krystal burgers now?" Joey wanted to know.

"I think we will, " Coco said, still shaking some. And this time we'll order everybody some ice cream. I think I'll have some, too."

"Yea!" we yelled.

I'm embarrassed to say I didn't know there was a Parthenon anywhere except Nashville until ninth grade, when Mrs. Sims, my Latin teacher, went off on a tangent one day talking about the one in Athens, Greece.

She claimed the Greeks had built a Parthenon, too. I wasn't the only one who hadn't heard of the "other" Parthenon. Turned out nobody else in my class had ever heard such a thing either.

Copycats, I thought.

16

Roadkill

We did a lot of praying on Sunday. Most of the time that was sufficient. But, from time to time, it came in handy on a regular old weekday . . .

The Bradley Smiths' driveway, paved and guarded on both sides by waist-high rock walls, wound its way from the Big Road around the side of the hill and up to the house in a series of steep switchbacks. Coco drove the Toad up and down that driveway several times a week. Most of the time she'd pull up in the paved turnaround area just below the Bradley Smiths' house and let us out or honk for us to come on and go home.

But sometimes she'd stay and visit with Mrs. Bradley Smith, and when she did, she always put on the parking brake and shifted the Toad into park before getting out of the car. Coco was scared to death that she'd forget to take those precautions and one of us boys would take an unsupervised joyride into an accident of mammoth proportions. If you'll remember, it was the fifties, and accidents—particularly automobile accidents—were commonplace.

The fact that Mr. Bradley Smith's new riding lawn mower had once backed its riderless way down that drive, jumped the wall, and ended up on its side in the woods was sufficient warning to anybody who'd heard the story. The Bradley Smiths told it so often that we could recite it from memory. And it caused Mr. Bradley Smith to put a handmade sign on their garage door:

CAUTION!
PUT CAR IN PARK AND APPLY PARKING BRAKE

Well, I guess you know what's coming. On a fateful Friday afternoon in April of '59, Coco parked the Toad in the turnaround as usual. As she honked the horn, she heard me screaming from the stone patio out behind the Bradley Smiths' house. I had taken a nasty spill and buckets of blood were pouring from my knee.

Coco didn't rush. She was accustomed to almost-daily injuries involving copious blood flow. But she did get out of the Toad and head up the steps to see whether my injury was as life threatening as it sounded.

And that's when Junior Bradley Smith lost interest in my injury, glanced down at the Toad from the patio, and started waving his arms, trying to say something. He couldn't get any words to come out. He didn't really need to. The look on his face and the arm waving were sufficient to cause everybody in attendance at my near-death experience, including me, to look down to the turnaround, where the Toad was rolling backward, in slow motion, but gathering speed. There was nothing to do but watch.

The Toad wandered toward the rock wall and hugged it close

while it scraped its way slowly down the drive. A loud metal-bending noise signaled removal of the fake wood paneling on the driver's side. It came off in one long piece and curled up at both ends like a giant wood shaving.

Coco and Mrs. Bradley Smith cupped their hands over their mouths (as if that was somehow an appropriate response) while metal on rock reverberated off the hillsides up and down our little valley. You could imagine Mrs. Whitley and Mrs. Mallory and Mrs. Witherspoon all out on their porches standing on tiptoes, peering up the Hollow, straining to see what was making that awful racket.

We McLeod boys, plus Junior and Possum, watched enthralled as the Toad bounded from one rock wall to the other, leaving side-view mirrors and chrome fenders and bits of fake wood in its wake, until it gathered up all the speed it could muster in a grand finale and went over the wall, pinballed off several big oak trees, flipped onto its side, and slid down the bank into Moccasin Creek, where it came to rest on its roof.

It was a great show.

For the longest time we stared at the Toad, sad that it was dead but savoring the memory of its colossal crash. And then we all turned to look at Coco to see if it was okay to cheer.

It was not okay.

As I've said before, Coco had bright red hair and freckled skin to match. We knew she was susceptible to sudden mood swings, which in our experience were mostly negative. We didn't know whether she was going to cry or yell or what, but we were pretty sure there would be some major eruption.

There wasn't. After she pulled her hands down from her mouth, she asked Mrs. Bradley Smith if she could borrow her phone to call the towing company to come pull the Toad from the creek and haul it away, which she did.

Then she walked all the way down the driveway, climbed over the rock wall, and picked her way down to the creek to find her purse. Surprisingly, it lay, muddy but intact, on the creek bank next to the wreckage.

After one last look at the Toad, Coco turned and walked back to the driveway and down toward the Big Road, telling us boys to fall in behind her for the march back to our house.

We begged and pleaded to stay for the tow truck, which promised to be the highlight of the show—the final act in our tragedy—but she said we needed to get home, all of us together, to call Dad and deliver the news. She told Mrs. Bradley Smith that she'd call him before he headed home from his office, so he'd have plenty of time to digest things. Mrs. Bradley Smith nodded and then Coco added that, to be on the safe side, Mrs. Bradley Smith should call the police if she didn't see any of us boys for a few days. That would be a sure sign of mass murder—our rotting bodies, bound and gagged, strewn about our house.

When we got home, Coco marched us into the parental bedroom. She sat down on the bed and gathered us all close around her. We bowed our heads. Coco said a little prayer. She asked God for forgiveness. Said she'd be more careful next time if He'd keep Dad from killing her, and us, too. "Help us, O Lord," she said.

"Even though we're just Methodists," Ricky added.

We all said, "Amen."

Coco dialed Dad's office. Sue Ellen, one of the nurses, answered and Coco asked her to get my dad and tell him to go into his office and close the door, so as not to disturb the staff or patients any more than necessary.

After a while, we heard Dad pick up the phone, whereupon Mom said that before she told him why she was calling, she wanted him to know that all five of us boys with our tender ears were sitting safely beside her on the bed, and he probably had a goodly number of patients in his waiting room who considered him a compassionate man with a decent bedside manner, and he should think about those things before he started yelling.

Things were quiet around our house that night, Dad being even less talkative than usual. It was the kind of quiet that caused us boys to do our chores without being asked and otherwise play quietly in our rooms. The next day, while Dad simmered, Coco made his favorite sandwich—toasted cheese and onion. Dad couldn't resist them. Way better than an olive branch.

And so, by Saturday afternoon the smoke stopped pouring from Dad's ears and his eyes lost their glassy stare. On Sunday after church, we all piled into Dad's car and went shopping for a brand-new 1959 lime-green Ford Country Squire station wagon with fake wood paneling, which we found, acquired, and christened the Tadpole.

A Coco rule: Whether you like it or not, you'll take a bite. It doesn't matter what *it* is. It doesn't matter what *it* looks like. It doesn't matter what *it* smells like. You are going to take a bite. And you are not going to hold your nose, or gag, or say anything bad about *it*.

So, I'm suggesting you try this sandwich before you decide you don't like it. We kids lined up at the oven door for 'em, right next to Dad.

Coco's Toasted Cheese and Onion Sandwiches

Serves 4

Ingredients
½ cup minced sweet onion

2 cups sharp Cheddar cheese, freshly grated

¼ cup mayonnaise

8 slices white bread, crusts removed

COMBINE onion, grated cheese, and mayonnaise in a medium mixing bowl. Spread onto four of the bread slices and put the other bread slices on top. Cut the sandwiches on the diagonal. Place the sandwich halves on a baking sheet and place under the broiler until toasted on one side. Flip sandwiches and toast on the other side.

GOOD . . . Really good!

17

On the Road
Big Timber, Montana

I'm headed to Buffalo, Wyoming, and the Occidental Hotel—famous for its bar and bison steak dinners. It's a long drive, so I stopped here in Big Timber, Montana (pop. 1,800), for lunch at Cole Drugs. I'm craving a grilled cheese sandwich and a tall glass of lemonade.

For almost twenty years, Annie and I vacationed with our girls at the Boulder River Ranch, south of here. And every year we stopped for fresh-squeezed lemonade at Cole Drugs before wending our way down valley. This old drugstore is a special place.

Back in its day, the Boulder River Ranch was a guest ranch without guest-ranch amenities—no cowboys singing around the campfire, no hot tub, no tennis courts, and no cold plunge unless you wandered down to the nearby river and jumped off the bank. Cabin walls were no impediment to fresh mountain air and we didn't have to worry about the kids' breaking things because most everything was already broken. But plentiful food was served family style in the dining hall and the company was good. We vacationed with the same families year after year and, over the years, became one extended family—what we still call the Boulder River Clan.

Two days from now, I'll spend a night with the Columbia, Missouri, branch of the clan. Charlie will barbecue his signature ribs. Millie, an unrepentant health nut, will bring something green. Alice will serve her famous apple pie (the one with the Cheddar cheese). Ted and I will contribute scintillating conversation. And we'll eat our way through the evening.

I'm looking forward to it.

But now, it's time for lunch . . .

At the drugstore, I took a stool at the counter, next to a short, plump, balding fellow, all decked out in a silver-colored jogging outfit, fancy running shoes, and a Seattle Mariners baseball cap—not what you'd call normal Big Timber attire. He was hunched over his laptop, scribbling numbers on the back of a napkin.

"Hi, name's Sam." I stuck out my hand. "What're you doin'?"

"Name's Rudy." He took my hand but didn't look up. "I'm tallying my sins."

"Those are some mighty big numbers. Looks like you're going to hell."

"Yeah." Rudy grinned. "Probably am. Got a Web site here that calculates the calories in restaurant food. I'm recording my calories for the day. Doc says I need to pay attention."

"Really? That's interesting," I perked up. "My doctor's singing the same tune. While you're at it, could you look up macaroni and cheese? I had some for dinner last night. It's too late to worry over it, but I've been wondering . . ."

"Sure," Rudy said. "Give me a second . . . macaroni and cheese . . . seven hundred and fifty calories a serving."

"Holy cow!" I said.

"How much did you eat?" Rudy asked.

"More than I should have. What's it say about carrot cake?"

"Probably nothing you want to hear." Rudy typed and waited. "It's even more—eight hundred calories a slice."

"Holy moly!" I said. (Actually, that's not *exactly* what I said.) "You've got to be kidding!"

About that time, Brenda the Waitress showed up and asked what I was having for lunch.

"Misgivings," I said. "I'll have a glass of water. Make that a *small* glass of water."

Rudy was still scribbling numbers. "Want to know anything else before I shut this baby down?" he asked.

"No . . . well . . . now that I think of it, how about barbecued ribs and apple pie, the kind with Cheddar cheese?"

"They're off the chart," Rudy speculated. "Yeah, ribs are over a thousand calories. This says thirteen hundred calories a serving. And the pie's eleven hundred calories a slice."

I was stunned.

"Where in the world have I been?" I said. "I had no idea . . ."

All of a sudden my upcoming dinner at the Occidental Hotel was looking more like a side salad than a bison steak and fries, and losing a few pounds before the social was looking hopeless.

Back in the car, my cell phone was beeping—a text message from my youngest daughter, Marshall.

Marshall's an assistant zookeeper in Tacoma, Washington. She's an animal lover like her mom and teaches zoo visitors about birds, snakes, and spiders while a tarantula crawls through her hair and a baby boa wraps itself around her neck. Kids squeal. Moms cringe. The audience loves it. It's the kind of job that makes me wonder whether she's really my daughter.

Here's the message:

HAVE FUN AT THE REUNION AND TELL COCO I SAID HI ☺ BUT DON'T FORGET MOM ☺ SHE'S WAY BETTER THAN SOME OLD GIRLFRIEND!!! OMG, MOM'S THE BEST!!!!!!

18

Beyond the Edge of the World

All this driving reminds me of McLeod family trips. Actually, I
shouldn't call them trips . . .

We McLeods went on expeditions, not trips. The word *trip* doesn't
begin to convey the enormity of the undertaking.

Our expeditions, in and of themselves, were not unusual. During
the fifties, Americans hit the road in staggering numbers. We traveled
crumbling, potholed back roads and new, four-lane interstate high-
ways divided by great, wide median strips—icons of America's vast-
ness. Names like Waffle House and Stuckey's were household words.
There were a lot of us on the road.

Expeditions started with provisioning. Whether we were taking
a weekend trip or going on a four-week trek, the provisioning was
much the same: we loaded the Toad (or the Tadpole) until its rear end
bumped the pavement.

On the morning of an expedition, Dad headed to the hospital a little earlier than usual to get out of the house and out of Coco's way. Coco was always a busy lady, but on the morning of an expedition she turned into a whirling dervish. She herded us boys into one of our bedrooms, lined us up next to our suitcases, and gave us a list of the things we were to pack—two clean blue jeans, four clean T-shirts, four clean pairs of underwear, etc. The word *clean* appeared in every line. The list covered us head to toe.

At the end of the list, she wrote: "NOBODY LEAVES THIS ROOM FOR ANY REASON UNTIL I HAVE INSPECTED ALL FIVE SUITCASES. DON'T EVEN ASK!"

We stayed in the room. We even attempted packing for a while. Coco eventually reappeared, shook her head, begged the Good Lord for patience, and packed for us like we knew she would.

Then she sent us away. Far away.

Coco made stacks of tuna sandwiches on Wonder bread and slipped each one into a waxed-paper sandwich bag. She dumped several hundred sweet gherkins into a large plastic bag. She hauled extra-large bags of potato chips and Oreo cookies from the pantry. She loaded the big cooler with ice, threw in the Nehi orange sodas, and packed the sandwiches and pickles on top of the bottles so as to keep them out of the ice, where they'd get soggy. Soggy sandwiches caused Harry to gag.

Half an hour before departure time, Dad came home to make his potted meat sandwich, a processed mess of minced meat and offal from some unidentified animal that looked and smelled like you-know-what. Mom couldn't stand the stuff. Said it made her gag. Harry, too. So Dad made his own sandwich and inserted it into a separate bag so it wouldn't contaminate the other food in the cooler.

And then we all went out to load the station wagon. The cooler, the grocery bag full of chips and Oreos, a box full of car games, and the first-aid kit all went on the floor of the Toad at Coco's feet.

Dad folded down the third row of seats and stuffed a double-bed mattress into the Way Back. Suitcases, blankets, pillows, and various toys surrounded the mattress. There were grocery bags full of towels in case we got wet, hooded sweatshirts in case we got cold (even though we already had sweaters on), an empty Folgers coffee can with a plastic lid, and the booze box—a special briefcaselike travel aid that held bottles of J&B Rare Scotch and Jack Daniel's Sour Mash whiskey, plus cocktail paraphernalia like a shot glass, highball glasses, mixers, and cocktail napkins. On top of the car, Dad filled the Toad's flimsy luggage rack with the rest of our gear, covered it with a tarp, and tied it down.

Once the car was loaded, Dad took the wheel, we kids jumped in the backseat (all five of us), and Coco headed back into the house to make sure she'd unplugged the iron, or unloaded wet clothes from the washing machine, or locked the back door, or whatever. Before every expedition, Coco disappeared into the house to check on something.

She stayed in there until Dad couldn't take it anymore and did the unthinkable. He honked the horn. We boys moaned. We knew what that meant. It meant that Coco would not be coming anytime soon. That honk sealed our fate. We sat in the car and waited her out. If Dad's temper didn't prompt him to honk again, Coco waited the necessary few minutes to prove that she wasn't at anybody's beck and call, made a prolonged show of locking the door behind her, and strolled nonchalantly to the car with a big smile on her face.

As soon as her bottom settled into the front seat, Dad zoomed off down the driveway and up the Big Road at breakneck speed to make up the time we'd lost. A chill descended on the Toad. Nobody spoke for several minutes, and then somebody farted and the silence was broken and all was forgiven.

About five minutes into the expedition, Mikey started his Coco-I'm-hungry mantra. And Coco started her it's-not-time-for-lunch retort. This went on for about fifteen minutes until Dad's nerves frayed for the second time. Then and only then did Coco retrieve a few sandwiches from the cooler and toss them in our direction.

Feedings posed a dilemma for Coco. If she didn't feed us, we whined until we drove Dad to the edge of madness. Coco was so accustomed to our whining that she hardly heard it, but Dad, accustomed to the relative peace of intensive care, couldn't handle whining. It drove him homicidal.

And if she did feed us—mostly foods full of the carbohydrates we craved—we buzzed on sugar highs and started pounding each other, another thing that drove Dad to consider unspeakable atrocities.

The trick was to delay feeding us until steam escaped from Dad's ears (just short of the homicidal stage) and then feed us in measured doses to keep our blood-glucose levels under control.

We played the alphabet game. Easy, until one of us "got to Q." Whoever spotted a Quaker State sign first got the Q and went blazing through the rest of the alphabet until he got to X while the rest of us waited for the next Quaker State sign. Anyone claiming to have seen an X was automatically called down for cheating. That started a yes-I-did and no-you-didn't battle that generally ended in the first time-out of the expedition. Coco sent one of us crawling over the backseat to the mattress to cool off.

Dad, both hands on the wheel and a grimace on his face, drove on. He hated to stop unless we needed gas. At the first gas stop, he begged us all to go to the bathroom. Mikey staunchly refused, saying he didn't have to go. Dad said it was a long way to wherever we were going and WE'RE NOT STOPPING AGAIN UNTIL WE GET THERE.

All of us, except Mikey, knew what that meant. Mikey never caught on.

Back in the car and headed down the highway, Coco handed out more tuna salad sandwiches and Nehi orange sodas. Then came potato chips and sweet gherkins. And finally, the Oreo cookies.

It is still one of my favorite meals.

Approximately ten minutes after we'd eaten our fill, Mikey said he had to pee.

You could have cut the silence with a butter knife. For the fourth time on our expedition, Dad prepared to strangle someone, and it wasn't necessarily Mikey he had in mind. We got the feeling that any one of us would do.

It happened on every McLeod expedition like clockwork. Coco was prepared. She waved her arm in the direction of the Way Back and summoned up the Folgers coffee can. She invited Mikey to climb into the front seat, where he stood facing the open road between Coco and Dad, unzipped, pulled out his little thing, and peed buckets into the can.

On most trips, Coco put the plastic top on the pee can and stowed it at her feet until we stopped again where she could dispose of the pee in the bathroom. We engaged a running debate whether it was appropriate for Coco to dispose of boy pee in a girls' toilet but the debate ended abruptly when Coco offered to let one of us boys carry that warm pee can into the boys' bathroom for emptying. End of discussion.

Once, while crossing the Tennessee River on a trip to Jackson, with all the windows rolled down for maximum ventilation, Coco decided to dispose of Mikey's pee before we reached our next stop. She didn't have her thinking cap on.

She pulled the plastic lid off the can and nonchalantly tossed its contents out the window while we sped along at sixty or more miles per hour. The air that pee was riding on came barreling into the backseat at, you guessed it, sixty miles per hour. I got soaked; Joey got wet; Ricky suffered some collateral damage; and everybody else laughed so hard they cried.

After endless hours of driving, we arrived at our destination. Dad breathed an enormous sigh of relief before bolting from the driver's seat to open up the Way Back and pull out the booze box. He hurried to the nearest sink—whether hotel or motel—where he mixed a scotch and water for himself and a whiskey sour for Coco.

Coco sent us boys off with a handful of dimes to find the nearest soda machine. We could buy whatever we wanted, as long as we took a long time doing it.

19

Eat Your Chicken Tails

*Not a summer passed without a monthlong visit in Jackson, Tennessee.
It was our second home. Those extended visits were good for us boys
and Coco and Dad. At the time, I thought they were also good for our
Jackson relatives. But now I wonder . . .*

Chasing after us eleven months of the year was enough to create a
willingness in Coco to give us up for a while. Every summer she carted
us off to Jackson to visit the relatives for as long as they'd take us.

About halfway along in our journey, Coco pulled over at a roadside picnic table on the east end of the Tennessee River Bridge. The
same spot every year. We knew the place well. We piled out of the car
and ran straight to the water's edge, where we skipped rocks off the
river's muddy brown surface while Coco laid out the tuna salad sandwiches and orange sodas.

Once the feeding was over, we were off again—over the Tennessee River Bridge into West Tennessee, through endless fields of cotton, corn, tobacco, and soybeans, into downtown Jackson.

Back then, Jackson was a rural farming community, hoping to become something more but not working very hard at it. Aside from a Piggly Wiggly, an Esso filling station, a five-and-dime, a courthouse, two churches (one Methodist and one Baptist), and a good many cinder-block barbecue establishments, there wasn't much to it.

Our first stop was the parsonage, where we'd spend a few days with our Jolley grandparents, Grandmother and Grandy, who lived about a mile from our McLeod grandparents. Long before we arrived, Grandmother stacked oatmeal cookies in a big tin on the kitchen table and stocked her refrigerator with milk.

After a short visit with Grandmother, Coco kissed us each good-bye and delivered a litany of instructions, which mostly boiled down to "Don't torture the relatives and don't wipe your nose with the back of your hand." Then she drove off looking sad but waving vigorously, and probably smiling inside about all the things she was going to do on her extended vacation from mothering.

While visiting our Jolley grandparents, we went to the Methodist church where Grandy was the preacher.

He was a giant of a man and the finest of Jolley specimens. Three-quarters bald, he combed a few well-oiled strands of coal-black hair over his shiny head. A hearing aid that looked like a wad of Silly Putty filled his meaty right ear. It hummed like an idling Hoover and whistled erratically, like it was calling the dogs from over in the next county. Grandy was the only one who couldn't hear it and seemed surprised when, right in the middle of a sermon, the churchgoers clapped their hands over their ears in unison and winced like they were getting their teeth drilled.

The air shuddered when Grandy blew his nose, something he did every few minutes (either bad allergies or a bad habit). He blew into his handkerchief and then absentmindedly wiped his glasses with it. He was forever holding his glasses up to the light, wondering why they weren't coming clean.

Grandy didn't talk like a normal human being. He boomed, hefting each word onto a pedestal and letting it sit there a little too long before replacing it with another. As a consequence, he was a long, plodding sermon maker. Several times during the service, we boys whispered down the pew, pestering Grandmother Jolley to tell us how much longer Grandy was going to torture us. We loved the jowly guy, but not because we admired his preaching.

Grandmother Jolley, wearing her basic-black high-collared church dress, sat primly proper in the pew, attempting to ignore us while listening dutifully to Grandy's sermon. That was the only time we ever saw her out in public.

When she wasn't in church, she, like my grandmother Mimi, was in the kitchen—baking, boiling, and broiling in a bibbed apron decorated with buttercups. Half spectacles resting comfortably on the bridge of her prominent nose, a hairnet holding her blue-gray hair in a tight bun on the back of her head, she hovered over a dog-eared cookbook propped against a tub of lard while she rolled out biscuit dough or filled cupcake tins with yellow cake batter. Collards simmered in the pressure cooker on the stove. Unshucked corn rested in a neatly stacked pile on the kitchen counter. Fresh-picked figs, just washed and rinsed, drained in the sink.

Unlike Grandy, Grandmother went about her life quietly—mostly unseen and unheard. She prided herself on her cooking and quilt making, letting the work speak for itself. Only rarely did Grandmother Jolley get riled up, but when she did, she'd take the big meat cleaver from its hook on the walk-in pantry wall, hack some just-plucked fryer into small pieces, wipe the blood and guts from her blade, take a deep breath, and mutter, "Now, that's better."

Following church, the shaking of hands, and the old-lady-pinching-of-cheeks, Grandmother loaded us grandkids into her basic-black Chevy sedan—the one that matched her church garb—and hauled us back to the parsonage for Sunday dinner. Grandy stayed at church until the stragglers cleared the pews, but he did not linger. He was not a man who missed many meals.

Grandmother served Sunday dinner in the dining room on her great-grandmother's antique dining table, which seated ten comfortably and up to fourteen uncomfortably. She set the table with inherited rose-patterned china, carefully polished silver, and fine crystal water glasses. She even trusted us with neatly ironed white linen napkins. That was unusual because she normally stuffed well-used kitchen towels into the tops of our T-shirts and fed us boys at the kitchen table, where we were less likely to do irreparable damage to treasured family heirlooms.

Grandy prayed over Sunday dinner until Grandmother politely cleared her throat, reminding him that it was Sunday, the grandkids were getting restless, and we'd already done enough praying to last a lifetime.

We passed our plates to Grandmother and fidgeted while she spooned up her famous chicken and rolled dumplings. Once everybody was served, Grandmother raised her fork—a bit of etiquette signaling that it was finally time to hunker down to some serious eating.

We kids could demolish a pot of dumplings but we were no match for Grandy, who'd been practicing for fifty or sixty years. He inhaled everything on his plate, passed his plate back to Grandmother, and in his most Methodist of preacher voices, formally requested that she spoon the chicken tail onto the edge of his plate along with another generous helping of dumplings.

The fatty heart-shaped tail rested on the lip of his dinner plate while Grandy downed another mountain of gravy-covered dumplings. As he slurped them up, he talked to the chicken tail: "Once I have eaten this lovely plate of Kate's fine dumplings, I'm coming for you, little chicken tail . . . You succulent little thing . . . I'm going to pick you up gently and admire you for a while . . . And then I'm going to put you in my mouth and chew you up good and taste every little bit of you before swallowing you down . . . Just wait right there while I finish my dumplings . . . And don't you worry your little head . . . I'm not going to forget you." And then, with his fat fingers, he picked the tail up, plopped it into his cavernous mouth, and chomped down on it with great gusto—tailbone and all. He made a big show of wiping his entire face with his napkin and then smiled at us boys.

"That was a fine meal, Kate," he said. "But I don't know where my manners went. Next time, I'll make sure one of you boys gets the tail."

We took that as a threat.

"Mighty fine. Mighty fine," he went on. "Now, what kind of cake are we having for dessert, my dear Kate? I'd love an oatmeal cookie with a scoop of your homemade peach ice cream on the side. How about you boys? And then why don't we all take a nap? I feel one coming on."

Grandmother Jolley's Chicken and Rolled Dumplings

Serves 4

Ingredients

For the chicken:
1 whole chicken, quartered
2 celery stalks, cut into 3-inch pieces
2 carrots, cut into 3-inch pieces
1 medium onion, quartered
1 bay leaf

4 cups canned, low-salt chicken broth

4 cups cold water

1 teaspoon freshly ground black pepper

1 teaspoon kosher salt

For the dumplings:

2 cups all-purpose flour

2 teaspoons baking powder

1 teaspoon kosher salt

½ cup Crisco

½ cup milk

reserved chicken stock

For the gravy:

4 tablespoons butter

4 tablespoons all-purpose flour

3 cups reserved chicken stock

1 tablespoon flat-leaf parsley, chopped fine

⅛ teaspoon freshly ground nutmeg

½ teaspoon freshly ground black pepper

½ teaspoon kosher salt

PREPARE THE CHICKEN:

PLACE the chicken pieces in a large pot, and add the celery, carrots, onion, bay leaf, chicken broth, water, pepper, and salt. The chicken should be covered by the liquid. If it's not, add enough water to cover. Cover the pot and slowly bring to a simmer. Simmer gently for two hours, skimming foam from the surface periodically.

REMOVE the chicken from the pot and set aside to cool. Strain the stock and skim the fat from the stock's surface. Rinse the pot. Return the chicken stock to the pot and keep warm over low heat.

ONCE the chicken has cooled, remove the bones and skin and cut into chunky (two-inch) pieces.

PREPARE THE DUMPLINGS:

WHILE the chicken is cooling, prepare the rolled dumpling dough. In a medium-size bowl, mix the dry ingredients. Add the Crisco and mix quickly with a fork or pastry blender until the flour resembles a coarse meal. (Do not substitute butter for the Crisco.) Add the milk and knead just enough to bring the dough together. Form the dough into a ball. Cover the dough with plastic wrap and refrigerate while you make the gravy.

PREPARE THE GRAVY:

IN a large saucepan, melt the butter over medium heat. Stir in the flour and cook over medium heat for about two minutes, whisking constantly. While whisking, slowly add three cups of the reserved chicken stock. Bring to a simmer and cook until thickened, just a few minutes. Add the parsley, nutmeg, salt, pepper, and chicken pieces.

FINISH THE DUMPLINGS:

WHILE the chicken is warming in the gravy, finish the rolled dumplings. Bring the remaining reserved chicken stock to a slow simmer. Roll out the dumpling dough to a one-eighth-inch thickness (very thin). Cut the dough into strips, one inch wide by three inches long. Drop the strips into the simmering stock one at a time. Do not overcrowd the pot. Cover and cook at a simmer, without removing the lid, for eight minutes, or until tender but not falling apart. Remove the dumplings with a slotted spoon and add to the chicken and gravy.

SERVE warm and enjoy!

20

Whoppers

*After a couple of days, Grandmother Jolley loaded us into her car
and carted us off to visit our McLeod relatives. Grandmother looked
somewhat relieved as she waved good-bye and drove away . . .*

Grandmother and Grandy dealt with us for two, maybe three days
before they ran out of steam and shuttled us off to the McLeod side of
the family. We tagged along with Granddaddy McLeod to his woodworking hobby shop, where he made baseball bats for us on his lathe
while Mimi and Wiese cooked huge quantities of food for our supper.

Mimi served biscuits and sausage gravy at every meal because
that's what Granddaddy liked with his buttermilk. It made no dif-
ference what meal it was or what else was on the table. We could be
eating Aunt Wiese's chicken deluxe and there'd still be biscuits and
sausage gravy on the table.

Granddaddy smacked his lips and talked with his mouth wide open so you could see the gravy and biscuits mixing. After every trip to Jackson, we returned home smacking and talking with our mouths full, driving Coco to distraction.

Granddaddy McLeod was a character. I know that now. But when I was a kid, he was just a grandpa.

He always looked like he was about to break into a smile, and laughed out loud at the most ordinary things. We quizzed him about what was so funny, but he rarely said.

Like Grandy Jolley, he could be loud—particularly when he was railing against Methodists, or the evils of drink, or Commies. But he could be very sweet—hugging tiny Mimi from behind and tickling her while her rubber-gloved hands were busy at the sink. She'd squirm and say something like, "Now, Ira, you stop that. What will the grandchildren think?" And he'd laugh out loud and say, "They'll think they should go about grabbing women from behind and tickling 'em."

Granddaddy, Mimi, and Wiese lived together in what we called "a grandma house"—one of those small two-story redbrick homes with dark gray shutters, a slate roof, and a covered wood-slat porch that ran along the front of the house over to the rose garden. A dark green awning hung out over a boxwood hedge.

Summer evenings after supper, Granddaddy sat on the porch sofa and read the *Jackson Sun;* Mimi, wearing her apron, sat in her own green wicker chair with a big plastic tub of green beans or black-eyed peas or corn on the footstool in front of her. She'd work over the vegetables—snapping beans, shelling peas, shucking corn—while we threw rocks at the squirrels in the maples that lined the quiet, well-shaded street. When Wiese came out after cleaning up the dinner dishes, she sat next to Mimi in a straight-backed chair and helped her.

As the sun slid out of the sky and dusk settled onto the lawn, porch lights came on up and down the street as the neighbors came out to visit and watch the light change. Granddaddy called us up on the porch. We climbed up beside him on the sofa and he told us a story before bed.

Granddaddy told hair-raising tales full of spitting cobras, secret passages behind mahogany bookcases, and inscrutable wizards gazing into crystal balls. And of course, there were heroic little boys who found their way through great mischief to do something useful. Odd combinations of witches, dogs, broken-down cars, and peanut-butter sandwiches provided story decoration. The more unusual the array of places, characters, and props, the better.

Most of Granddaddy's tales scared us so bad we scrunched down between the sofa cushions looking for a place to hide—tales so scary we lay awake in our beds afraid to close our eyes for fear the wild-eyed loner looking for his golden arm would be on us as soon as we nodded off.

Mimi and Wiese listened, too. Even they were amazed at the unpredictable twists and turns in Granddaddy's stories and gasped when the hero escaped certain death at the hands of a deranged kindergarten teacher. They gave up warning Granddaddy that we were scared witless and weren't going to sleep. Granddaddy dismissed overprotectiveness with a twinkle in his eye and even scarier stuff. Warning Granddaddy only encouraged bad behavior.

Sometimes he let us help him with his story. And no matter how wild our tales or scary the villains, Granddaddy McLeod encouraged us to make them wilder and scarier. Sometimes the stories we made up with him scared us more than the ones he made up on his own. Then he'd wag his finger at Wiese and Mimi, saying it didn't matter whether he told scary tales or not. We were perfectly capable of scaring ourselves witless. And then he'd laugh that strange laugh of his, slap his knee, and say, "Now, that was a whopper."

Those were glorious nights. By the time we went to bed, the crickets were chirping and the fireflies were flitting about, and no matter how hard we tried to stay awake to be sure we didn't get hacked to death by the loner searching for his arm or bitten by something venomous, we nodded off, lulled to sleep by the cool breeze coming in through the open window.

21

White Sauce

Our McLeod relatives loved us for one night, put up with us for a second night, and dumped us back on Jolleys well before noon on the third day . . .

Aunt Irma, Coco's older sister, and her husband, Uncle Pete, lived on a sprawling farm about fifteen miles east of Jackson where they took us in for several weeks each summer. They were brave and patient people—personality traits that were easier to pull off in a place where there was an inexhaustible supply of adventures that kept us boys mostly on the back forty, and where there was Mamie, an old black woman who lived with my aunt and uncle. Mamie took charge of us like we were her own. She called herself our summer mother, and she was.

■ ■ ■

The farm was a Civil War survivor. Aunt Irma told us eye-popping stories about how Uncle Pete's grandparents had opened up the farmhouse as an infirmary for the Confederate army, and how a nighttime raid by Yankees had left bullet holes in two of the upstairs doors—holes big enough that you could stick your index finger through them. Faded photos in wooden frames decorated the walls—stern-looking men wearing the uniform of the Confederacy and primly proper women in dark dresses buttoned up to the chin. My aunt could tell you the place of every one of those folks on Uncle Pete's family tree and more than you'd want to know about each of them. A locked glass case full of Confederate rifles, swords, and medals stood at the far end of the upstairs hallway.

The two-story white clapboard house had a double-decker porch running across the front and around the corner to the kitchen door. Porch ceiling fans turned day and night. The main-floor porch featured two swings, lush potted ferns, and an eclectic assortment of rocking chairs and small tables (for setting down your lemonade glass). The bead-boarded porch ceiling was painted light blue to discourage wasps from constructing nests up there. A big plastic tub of string beans waiting to be strung and snapped always sat on one of the rocker seats.

Inside there was a living room we rarely entered, a dining room that barely contained the harvest table where we took our noon meal, and a high-ceilinged kitchen with a wood-fired stove and a breakfast table with seating for ten.

Behind the kitchen Mamie had a tiny self-contained apartment that opened onto the kitchen porch and looked as if it had been tacked onto the house as an afterthought.

Upstairs were the bedrooms—one huge room where my aunt and uncle slept, and two bedrooms across the hall where we kids were housed. One of our bedrooms opened onto the upstairs porch, where there were a couple of steel-framed beds that provided open-air comfort on the hottest, most humid of summer nights. If we promised not to hang over the balcony railing, we were permitted to drag our blankets and pillows out onto the porch, where we could set up camp for the night.

Only one of us ever leaned too far over the porch railing. Ricky fell into the sticker bushes headfirst. That was the last time any of us played on the railing. We preferred to learn our lessons the hard way, but we did learn.

There were animals everywhere. Cats lived in the barn and under the back porch; dogs rolled in the dusty bare spots out by the chicken coop; chickens pecked their way around the base of the gargantuan oak tree that shaded the front of the house; and a cocky rooster strutted about, menacing everything in sight. We learned to steer clear of him.

There were pigs by the barn. The piglets were always escaping from the pen and trying to get into the kitchen. It was our job to catch and return them to their mother. Homer, a Shetland pony too wild to ride, munched on grass out in the pasture beyond the barn. On the far side of the pasture, a small pond brimmed with sunfish, bass, and snapping turtles. And beyond the pond, a dense forest of hardwoods and Southern pine made a good place to build a fort out of deadfall and mud bricks.

A showerhead and a pull chain hung from a cedar post just outside the kitchen door. That's where we were instructed to strip down before lunch—leaving our filthy clothes in a heap on the ground. Mamie made us scrub ourselves raw before she allowed us to run *nekkid* through the kitchen and up the stairs to find some clean clothes to put on.

I associated the farm with white sauce. Aunt Irma and Mamie each made slightly different versions. Aunt Irma threw in a bay leaf and some fresh thyme or chopped parsley or whatever other herb was growing in the small garden by the kitchen steps. Mamie threw in a bay leaf and a little freshly ground nutmeg, saying she didn't understand why anybody'd put grass in their food. Aunt Irma just smiled.

We ate white sauce three meals a day—on biscuits for breakfast, on boiled new potatoes for lunch (what Uncle Pete called "dinner"), and again on boiled potatoes for supper. At breakfast, Mamie peppered her white sauce heavily and laced it with the pan drippings from our sausage patties. We got the mostly unadulterated version at lunch and dinner. We loved white sauce.

We spent afternoons on the side porch with Aunt Irma and Mamie—recovering from our lunch of fried chicken, lima beans, sliced tomatoes, corn on the cob, boiled potatoes with white sauce, corn bread with farm-churned butter, big glasses of milk, and a gigantic slice of Mamie's pie baked earlier in the morning—cherry, apple, peach, blackberry, strawberry, blueberry, or rhubarb. Life was good.

Afternoons on the porch were all about staying in the shade. We shelled peas, shucked corn, trimmed okra, sorted tomatoes and lined them up on the kitchen windowsill in order of ripeness. And then rearranged them by size. And then put them back in order of ripeness again. Mamie warned us all afternoon: "You chil'ern leave my 'maters be," and "Y'all makin' Mamie tired 'ith all that runnin' 'round," and "Harry, if you cut your han' off'n that knife, don' be botherin' Mamie with yo' blubberin'."

We ate our supper early—mostly cold and left over from lunch. Not only were Mamie and Aunt Irma worn out, but nobody wanted to fire up the stove in the heat of the day to cook anything. That was okay with us boys. We'd just eat another plate of cold potatoes with white sauce and head outside.

Summer evenings at the farm were about collecting fireflies in a quart-size Ball jar to light up the sleeping porch at night. We ate the watermelon Uncle Pete retrieved from the icehouse—big chunks sprinkled with a little salt from the shaker that sat all summer on the front-porch railing.

Mamie scolded us about dribbling watermelon juice down the fronts of our T-shirts and the mess we made spitting watermelon seeds at each other while we ran around the front yard. And then she lined us all up, stripped us *nekkid*, washed us head to toe with a garden hose, toweled us off, and sent us racing upstairs to get on our pajamas—our second washing of the day and the second pile of dirty clothes left on the ground.

Aunt Irma just smiled.

22

Talkin' to Jesus

Mamie was special—one of the great women who hovered over me . . .

I can't tell you where Mamie came from, or how she got to the farm, or much about her family. I only met one of her relations—a cousin named Pokey, who drove a wreck of a truck that he complained about more than he drove. Pokey came around pretty regularly to see Mamie and sometimes brought along barbecue in a red Coleman cooler. But he was always yelling at that truck, and my uncle was forever out there in the yard with him trying to get the thing running. Mamie said that truck labored under the "devil's own curse." She could get a little put out with Pokey and his truck.

I never knew Mamie's age. But she was old. She looked old, and she talked about her "ol' bones" whenever she got up from her rocking chair. She had what she called an "ol' woman crew cut" of tiny white curls all over her head. She wore clip-on pearl earrings that she fiddled with constantly. Her eyes were dark brown and half sunk into a face of wrinkles, but you could still see her dimples—she'd point them out to you; and she was always saying that I must be related to her because we both had dimples. I liked that.

The skin on her arms hung loose from her thin bones, deep folds of crusty skin where her elbows were supposed to be. She looked frail but wasn't; she could grab an out-of-control boy and jerk him to a halt just as easily as she could carry a giant pot of boiling potatoes from the stove to the sink, just as easily as she could chase down a chicken and lop off its head before the poor thing had any idea that it was "boun' for heaven above, amen."

Mamie wore her gray work dress every day and protected it from abuse with a full apron covered in small blue flowers, ruffled at the shoulders. She wore support-type leather shoes sometimes, but went barefoot the rest of the time. Whenever we sat out on the porch with Aunt Irma and Mamie, Mamie kicked off her shoes and wiggled her toes, saying that shoes "was the devil's own curse laid on ol' women." My aunt would smile and tell us boys to keep our shoes on—when we got to be Mamie's age, we could run around the farm barefoot, but not before.

Mamie called my aunt "Miss Irma" even though my aunt was married; and my aunt called Mamie "Miss Mamie." They were very formal that way. Sometimes we heard Mamie being bossy to our aunt: "Miss Irma, you go on an' git outta this here kitchen and outta my way." And Mamie waved her hands out in front of her like she was sweeping my aunt from the kitchen. And they both laughed and went on about their business.

And sometimes she bossed our uncle: "Mr. Pete, git yo'self back out on that porch in them mud boots and don't you dare be trackin' mud in my kitchen." And Uncle Pete went back out onto the porch and took off his boots. Mamie owned the kitchen.

Another thing about Mamie: she sang while she worked, as long as nobody else was around. Every morning we woke to Mamie's singing in the kitchen while she prepared our breakfast. Aunt Irma was already out in the garden collecting vegetables for lunch. Uncle Pete was off on his tractor early, as usual. And Mamie thought we were sleeping. But we weren't. We lay in our beds and listened to her singing about swinging low, and the angel on her shoulder, and going home to Jesus.

One day, I surprised Mamie in the kitchen and asked her what she was singing. She said, "Lawd, honey, I warn't singin'. I's jus' talkin' to Jesus."

Like all of the women who surrounded us, Mamie knew a lot of stuff. She taught us how to bait a hook with an earthworm and how to catch the giant grasshoppers hopping around in the field in front of the house. She showed us how to hook the hoppers and float them out on the farm pond, where big sunfish pounced on them. She knew how to clean those fish, roll them in flour, and fry them up for our breakfast. Mamie claimed the fish we caught out of the pond each summer made the best breakfast anybody ever thought up.

Mamie knew where the devil was at all times. On a walk back from the pond one morning with a stringer full of brightly colored sunfish, Joey spied a black snake slithering across the path ahead and pointed it out to the rest of us. Mamie jumped about ten feet backward, ran through the barn gate, and climbed up on an abandoned pig shed. She stood up there yelling for us boys to climb up beside her "quick as sparks so's the devil cain't git us."

Mamie had an understanding of living that comes with a lot of it. Unlike most, Mamie accepted the folks who graced her days without judgment. She wasn't trying to fix anybody.

I remember once running into the kitchen to tell Mamie that Mikey was missing. The rest of us had been so engrossed in tormenting a hive of ground-dwelling bees that we hadn't noticed him wandering off. As I burst through the kitchen porch door, there was Mikey sitting in Mamie's lap, tears running out of his eyes.

I asked what was wrong and Mamie said Mikey was feeling a little blue—just a touch sad because he was homesick. That got us off on a discussion about homesickness and somewhere in the middle of all that talk I asked Mamie if she ever got sad.

"Sometimes . . . sometimes I's sad . . . but never for long," Mamie said.

"So, what makes you sad, Mamie?" I pressed.

"Lawd, chile, ain't nothing make me sad. Nuthin' ever make a body sad. A person get to decide that. If you sad, or mad, or whatnot, it's 'cuz you choosin' to be. It be your choice. Don' never forget that."

23

Black Church

While we were hers, Mamie made sure we got our religion . . .

One Sunday each summer, we went with Mamie to her church. It wasn't anything like Aunt Irma's church. It was fun.

When we went to the white church, Aunt Irma made us sit in the front row. (Like Coco, she'd learned the trick from Grandmother Jolley.) The white church was a solemn sort of place, exciting only when the stiff-legged altar boy threatened to set fire to something other than the candles. Thankfully, that happened more often than the organist liked. She was forever looking up from the organ music, out over her glasses, frowning at him.

Otherwise, the white church was stern-looking choir members singing serious hymns from the pages of the official hymnal, a dour-looking preacher droning on about finding joy in Christ, and old ladies to smile at. We did not care much for Aunt Irma's church. Unfortunately, my aunt wasn't terribly interested in whether we liked it or not. We were going, whether we liked it or not.

When Mamie took us to her church, she wore a satiny lavender church dress, a purple hat the size of a hubcap, glistening white heels, and white gloves. Uncle Pete always commented on how nice she looked.

Pokey picked us up in his truck and squeezed us into the smallest rear seat you've ever seen—really just an open space behind the bench seat up front. Pokey helped Mamie, who was carrying a huge plate full of peanut-butter cookies, into the passenger seat, and then climbed in behind the wheel. He didn't have to start the truck because he'd never turned it off. Mamie saw to that. She instructed Pokey on when to pick us up (even though he already knew) and warned him to leave the truck running while we all piled in. She told us boys that she'd rather spend some time with Jesus than stare at Pokey's rear end while his head was stuck up under the hood of that truck trying to get it started again.

The black church was a tiny whitewashed concrete-block affair way off the highway down a road that was more potholes than pavement. We parked under the trees right next to the church and wandered through the tall weeds to the front door. Reverend Johnson, the pastor, made over us boys like we were his own. He gave us each a peppermint from his pocket while Mamie pretended to look the other way.

Folks inside the church laughed and talked so loud our ears rang. The ladies pinched our cheeks and the men knuckled our crew-cut heads. There were kids everywhere chasing each other and having a big time. It was a lively place.

But that was just the start. After a while, Reverend Johnson wandered down the aisle toward the front of the church shaking hands with everybody now seated in pews, and the din would peter away into silence. He stood at the front of the church, raised both of his big hands, and made a prayer to Jesus while we all sat quiet as we could be. He prayed for Jesus to come to our church and save us from the ways of the devil.

Right after the opening prayer, church ladies strolled up and down the main aisle handing out cardboard fans with a church saying on one side and a picture of Jesus on the other, while the Reverend Johnson made a joke about keeping cool with Jesus. We laughed politely and fanned ourselves vigorously all through the service.

Next came a hymn. There was no organ—just the voices of the three or four women and two men in the choir. The song started off slow but built to a crescendo that had us all swaying in our seats and some folks clapping along. Unlike the white church, this was a church where swaying in your seat was encouraged.

Reverend Johnson stepped into the pulpit as the hymn hit its high point and ended abruptly. The little church went silent—just the noise of fans fanning and the creaking of the old wooden pews under the considerable weight of some of the churchgoers.

Reverend Johnson started in on his sermon nice and slow with a soft voice. We knew what was coming. It was like feeling the growing rumble of a freight train underfoot long before the train comes barreling down on you. It was exciting.

Ever so slowly, the reverend's voice grew deeper and louder. Folks behind us started what Mamie called the "amen-ing." Reverend Johnson belted out a sentence about Jesus coming—in his mind's eye he could see Jesus now walking down the road toward our little church to gather up His children—and everybody, including us boys, said "amen."

And then the reverend belted out another vision of Jesus nearing the church and seeing the cars and trucks of His children parked under the shade trees—and everybody said, a little louder this time, "amen." And then Reverend Johnson raised his hands up high again and shut his eyes tight and said even louder that he could see our sweet Jesus stepping up to the door of the church preparing Himself to enter and greet all His children.

The choir erupted into a spiritual that everybody but us knew by heart, and the crowd joined in the singing as Reverend Johnson strode toward the door of the church, shaking hands with the men as he went and hugging the overjoyed ladies. He was going to let our Lord Jesus in.

Well, I'm here to tell you the place went crazy. Folks were singing themselves hoarse and screaming out their amens. Ultralarge women in big floppy hats and flashy high heels danced down the aisle to greet Jesus. Kids stood up in the pew seats to get a better view as the reverend opened the doors to the church so the invisible presence of Jesus could accompany him back down the aisle to the front of the church as a couple of parishioners passed out from the excitement of it all and had to be laid out on pew seats until they could recover.

Oh my, what fun it was—singing, clapping, dancing on the pew seats, and watching the show as that little church rocked on its foundation. White people did not know what they were missing.

On one of our trips to the farm, I remember asking Mamie why she couldn't come to the white church with us. She shook her head and said it "warn't nuthin' worth worryin' over"—that "we'd all end up in the same church on that day when our sweet Jesus came callin' us to heaven."

Amen.

24

A Red-Hair Moment

*Trips to Jackson were fine, but there came a day when Coco decided
we needed to see more of this world . . .*

Coco loved to travel, and thank goodness. Had it not been for her
wanderlust and gritty determination, we boys might never have seen
a ton of slobbering bull on a heifer.

"What are they doing, Aunt Irma? Is that cow taking him for a
piggyback ride?"

Or an old man masticating biscuits and sausage gravy with his
mouth wide open.

"How do you keep that mess in your mouth, Granddaddy?"

Or a minister talking to a chicken tail.

"Grandmother, you think that thing could hear him?"

Just think of all the important stuff we'd have missed.

Unfortunately, our travels took a toll on Coco. Getting us through an expedition was a lot like driving a mule team, except the driver pulled while the mules lounged in the wagon. Afterward, Coco was worn out.

It was a dreary Monday night in late winter—dark and drizzly. We'd spent another weekend in Jackson, visiting the relatives. It had been a particularly unpleasant adventure and Coco was showing the strain.

At dinner, after Dad said the blessing and before any of us could spin the lazy Susan, Coco banged her orange plastic tumbler with a butter knife. (Coco never banged her tumbler unless there was a problem.) We boys eyed each other nervously. Somebody was getting ready to *get it*.

"This has got to change," Coco said.

She was looking squarely at Dad, her eyes wide, no blinking.

It looked like Dad was going to *get it*.

"What's got to change?" Ricky piped up.

We all cringed, even Dad. Ricky had an uncanny knack for asking the wrong question at the wrong time. Reading Coco's body language was not his strong suit.

"Our trips," Coco replied in a frighteningly controlled way. She looked back at Dad.

Ricky had dodged a bullet.

"These boys are going to see something of the world and so are we," Coco said.

She paused, letting her declaration hang in the air for a few seconds, so it could sink in.

"But I can't get us there by myself. If I can't get some help from you, we're never going anyplace but Jackson, and after the debacle of a trip we just survived, we may never go there again, either."

Coco paused, waiting for Dad to say something.

He didn't.

That really made her mad.

She stabbed her place mat with her index finger. "I want us to take these boys to the beach. And New York City. And someday California. And who knows where else. And we're never going to any of those places if you don't get up off your butt and help me."

Holy moly! Coco said "butt." Saying "butt" was frowned upon in our house, mostly by Coco. While Coco would grudgingly agree that "butt" was not really foul language, it was, according to her, "not nice." So we weren't allowed to say "butt," and Coco never said "butt," but she'd just said "butt," and that's when we knew Dad was *really* going to *get it*.

We put our hands over our mouths and started to laugh, but Coco put on her don't-cross-me look and the merriment stopped. Coco was so mad she couldn't decide between screaming and crying. Her lips trembled. Tears welled up in her eyes but none spilled. She looked us over like we were a bunch of strangers.

Dad took a sip of his J&B Rare Scotch.

Her voice quavered. "If you won't get off your throne and help me get these boys some experience in this world outside this little valley and your daddy's damn Baptist church . . ."

Holy moly! Coco said "damn," which was unquestionably foul language. This was turning into a night to remember.

". . . I swear I'm going to an early grave and I'm leaving these hooligans with you. Let's see just how well you get along without me."

"But you'll miss us, Coco," Ricky said.

Jeez, when would the boy learn?

"No I won't," Coco shot back. Flames danced in her eyes now. The tears had boiled away. The quaver was gone from her voice.

"No I won't, young man, and you want to know why?"

She didn't wait for an answer.

"Because you and your brothers will be in heaven with me. Inside ten minutes after I'm laid in my grave, your father will go stark-raving mad and murder each and every one of you, and you'll all be coming to heaven to live with me . . ."

She paused again, letting the picture set in, then added in her most chilling voice, "Except your dad, and that's because he's going STRAIGHT TO HELL."

We were having the ultimate red-hair moment.

Coco did not go to her grave and nobody got murdered and Dad did not go to hell, so things didn't turn out as badly as they could have, but the rest of that evening was unusually quiet. I can't tell you what transpired between Coco and Dad behind closed doors that night or the next or the next, but the gloom lifted a few days later and Coco returned to us as her mostly normal self, ready to press her travel agenda with renewed enthusiasm.

A week or so later . . .

"We're going to the beach this summer!" Coco shrieked, dancing circles in the middle of the kitchen, bouncing Mikey on her shoulders. "I just got off the phone with your dad and we're all going to the beach! Well, actually he didn't say yes, but he didn't say no. And that usually means yes, so I'm taking it as yes—"

"What beach?" Joey asked. We'd seen beach pictures, but had no personal experience of one.

"St. Simons Island on the Georgia coast. We're going to stay in a cottage for two whole weeks right on the Atlantic Ocean and run barefoot in the sand and play in the waves and build sand castles and slather ourselves with baby oil and get a tan."

(Coco never tanned. Redheaded people don't tan, they freckle, and Coco freckled with the best of them.)

"We're going to see Beppy and Bob and their kids—Betty and Bart and Bob Jr. You're all about the same age and I just know you're going to love them and become best friends. I haven't seen Beppy in so many years. We were best friends while your dad and Dr. Bob were in medical school, and I can't wait to see her again. Oh, boys, what fun we're going to have . . ."

The twirling and dancing slowed. We could tell that another thought had come into Coco's head. She lowered Mikey to the floor, crouched down, and drew us into a circle around her like she wanted to tell us a secret.

"I know we can do this, boys." She was pleading now. "You boys will be good, won't you? I just know you will. We can do this if we put our minds to it."

She stopped to think for a minute.

"We'll practice. That's it. Somehow we'll practice. I don't know how yet, but we'll practice. You boys will learn to travel like little angels and we'll show your dad that you are ready to see some of this world."

Over the next several weeks, Coco was as creative and tenacious as we'd ever seen her, constantly tweaking her plans. Every obstacle Dad threw up, Coco tore to the ground. That is, until he threw up this one:

"Remember," he said, "Jackson is two hours away. Brunswick is ten. You've thought about that, haven't you?"

Oops.

Coco'd been so focused on being at the beach that she hadn't thought about how we were going to get there. She certainly hadn't considered what it would be like to travel with the five of us in the Toad for ten hours.

"Let me think about that," she said, looking like she was going to be sick. It took a week or so, but the ever-resilient Coco came up with what she declared a brilliant idea.

"Just hear me out," she started.

Dad was already shaking his head.

"We'll travel at night—all night—and share the driving. And take a big thermos of coffee. We'll fix up the mattress in the Way Back and take the sleeping bags. The boys will stay in the Way Back and sleep the whole way. I'll ride in the backseat with the cooler and sandwiches and the coffee can."

Dad was still shaking his head.

"And that's not all. We'll practice. Every Saturday night until we get it right, we'll go to the drive-in. We'll eat dinner in the car. The boys'll stay up through the cartoons. And when it gets dark, they'll go to bed in their sleeping bags in the Way Back while we watch the movie, and then we'll bring them home and carry them to their beds, and you'll see, they'll sleep like the dead all night long. I just know this is going to work."

She turned to us and put on her don't-you-dare-cross-me look.

"Won't it, boys?"

We nodded. "Yes'm," we said.

The cotton candy was, in retrospect, a bad idea. Before Mikey was done with it, he had cotton candy in his ear, on his hands and shirt, in Joey's hair, between the seat cushions, and all over the mattress in the Way Back—a mattress that had started out the evening dressed in an old but clean, blue fitted sheet.

While we boys watched Tom & Jerry on the big screen, spilled our 7UP—no Cokes in the car, boys—dropped half-eaten hot dogs on the floorboards, wiped mustard-covered hands on the mattress and each other, and dumped popcorn everywhere, Coco climbed back and forth between the backseat and the Way Back, wiping everything (including us) with a wad of napkins she'd soaked in the girls' bathroom.

Dad spent the evening taking us two at a time to the boys' bathroom. When he wasn't wiping a butt offered up by an innocent child hugging a urine-encrusted toilet seat, he sat motionless in the front seat of the Toad, jaws clenched, staring doggedly at *The African Queen* playing on the big screen in front of him. Had it not been for the sound of grinding teeth, you might have mistaken his pose for some sort of meditation practice.

The next morning before we went to church, Coco cheerfully served Dad a plate of fried eggs (over easy), country ham, and home-made biscuits—his favorite—while we boys snarfed down Krispy Kreme donuts and chugged our milk.

"That wasn't so bad, was it? We survived our first practice at the drive-in," Coco said brightly. "No worries, we'll get the hang of it, and we'll get better. You'll see. Want a fresh cup of coffee?"

Over the next few months we got better—not great, just better. I thought we'd never get there, but the second week of July finally arrived and we were on our way to the beach.

Driving at night through pouring rain took its toll. Dad drove while Coco slept. Then Dad slept while Coco drove. But they were both tuckered out.

Halfway along in our trek, Coco woke us saying we were stopping at Waffle House to get some coffee and breakfast—a place Dad knew from going to medical meetings in Atlanta.

"But it's dark," Harry said.

"Probably won't keep you boys from eating some waffles," Dad said.

"Yeah!" we said.

Coco passed sweatshirts and tennis shoes over the backseat.

"But I'm not cold," Joey said.

"Well, I am," Coco barked, blowing a strand of red hair from her face. "And I know best, so put your sweatshirts on."

"But—"

"End of discussion," Coco said.

Dad docked the Toad and we piled out into a warm Georgia night. The air was heavy, smelling of rain on hot pavement. Bright light poured through the big windows from inside the restaurant and glistened on the wet sidewalk. Water dripped from a downspout by the door.

The place was loud with the conversation of truck drivers in sleeveless T-shirts, late-shift nurses all in white, and factory workers in dark blue coveralls. Dad liked "rubbing elbows with real people" and settled onto a stool at the counter next to a guy hauling a load of furniture from North Carolina to Texas. We lined up beside him.

Huge metal pots and blackened skillets clattered. Smells of coffee brewing, waffles, and bacon filled the air. The waitresses knew everybody, talked loud enough to be heard in Chattanooga, and peppered the cook with orders. The tall waitress with the big blonde hair wanted to know where we lived and where we were going.

"So, why are you boys wearing sweatshirts? It's *hot as the devil* outside."

We rolled our eyes toward Coco.

Coco said she'd have another cup of coffee and eyed the counter like she was going to nap on it.

Dad ate scrambled eggs, toast, and bacon while we boys gorged on waffles covered in square pools of melted butter mixed with maple syrup. Coco ate some of Dad's eggs, but mostly drank her coffee and dabbed us with a wet towel she'd pulled from a sack in the Toad.

Before we left, the big-haired waitress filled Dad's thermos. Dad's trucker friend hoisted each of us into his cab and let us explore for a while before Coco herded us back into the Toad.

Dad took up his position behind the wheel, hot Waffle House coffee in his cup. Coco curled up on the backseat, said she didn't want to hear a peep from the peanut gallery, and went fast asleep.

Wandering the muddy sand flats of St. Simons Island at low tide was high adventure for us McLeod boys—landlubbers from the central Tennessee plateau. The flats stretched a half mile or more out to sea when the moon's invisible tug was strongest. Deep, dark channels meandered the flats, allowing the surf to run in and out. The ocean stretched to the horizon behind a fleet of net-dragging boats that plied the waters at the edge of the roiling surf.

Dr. Bob told us the boats were shrimpin' and showed us in a picture book how the nets were let out and hauled in, full of plump Georgia shrimp. "The very best shrimp in the whole world," he said, more than once.

He and Dad showed us how to stretch a seine net across a deep channel as the tide rushed out. We caught fat shrimp and all manner of baitfish as they scurried in the fast-moving current back to the sea and kept them in sand buckets full of seawater until they died.

We even jumped into the deep channels on car-tire inner tubes and rode the tide into oncoming waves. Dad and Dr. Bob let us wade into the waves and tumble in the surf, and they showed us how to catch a wave and ride it until it dumped us on our heads.

It was adventure like we'd never imagined.

Beppy and Coco read their beach books, chatted more than they read, knitted but never finished anything, worried about all the ways we kids could drown, and otherwise manned our beach camp—heavy canvas umbrellas, brightly colored beach towels and half-wet T-shirts hanging from the umbrella struts, sturdy canvas beach chairs with wooden armrests moved around under the umbrellas as the sun crossed the sky overhead, giant metal coolers, more towels laid out on the sand, picnic baskets, inner tubes, shovels, buckets of all shapes and sizes, and the rest of the mess that marked the beach territory we'd claimed for the day.

The moms took turns putting down their beach books, climbing out of their fully reclined chairs, shading their eyes with one hand, looking out to where we were playing, shaking their heads at the reckless behavior of the dads, waving madly with their free hand, and yelling at us, "You kids are out too far. Come on back in." Or at the dads, "Honey, you're letting the kids out too far. Y'all need to come on back in."

If it looked like the dads were letting us do something particularly stupid, they'd both get out of their chairs and yell.

Bob Jr., Betty, and Bart were our beach guides. They knew where to dig for fiddler crabs in the midday surf, where to find the white sun-bleached sand dollars among the dunes, and how to build elaborate sand castles.

They came with all the beach gear we landlocked Tennessee people had never acquired—sturdy, short-handled shovels made for serious digging, full-size aluminum buckets, real car-tire inner tubes for riding in the channels, heavy-duty floats, and a tire pump for blowing everything up.

We came with flimsy plastic shovels and buckets, thin-skinned plastic tubes with bikinied, pink baby hippos on them, and floats decorated with happy Disney characters—Mickey and Minnie and Goofy. All that stuff lay neglected next to the life jackets Coco bought us—fluorescent-orange ones suitable for floating fat babies in the shallow end of a blow-up pool.

When we first arrived, Betty, Bart, and Bob Jr. had looked at our stuff. "Who brought the baby toys?" Bart wanted to know.

It was embarrassing.

It happened late one afternoon as massive thunderheads built over the beach. A shark struck viciously, but silently, in the scary blue depths of a darkening channel—one we'd been playing in for days.

There was a sudden silver flash. The water erupted, then calmed. Oily red blood undulated on unseen currents in an ever-widening circle from the spot where, just a split second before, some unsuspecting baitfish had met his end.

Aside from the waves crashing farther out, the world went still. We kids stood next to the channel momentarily transfixed by the blood—watching it disperse in the inky-blue water. And then we ran—scared witless—in a terrified pack, back to the safety of the moms and the beach umbrellas that hovered over our vacation.

I sprinted ahead of my brothers and promised God I'd do anything He wanted—anything—if He'd let me live. I thought about what it'd feel like to have sharks ripping away chunks of flesh, knowing I was dying, wondering how long I'd suffer before my short, and seriously unfulfilled life passed into oblivion.

"I mean it, God," I yelled. "I'll do anything."

And then, as clear as any words were ever spoken, I heard somebody say, "Stop hitting your brothers."

"What?"

The words came again, louder this time: "STOP HITTING YOUR BROTHERS."

I didn't know where they came from. Was I making them up in my head? Was God talking to me?

I didn't have time to figure it out.

"Okay, okay," I yelled, on the verge of tears. "If You let me live, I'll never hit my brothers again. Ever. I mean it. I PROMISE."

We flew into beach headquarters, gasping for oxygen. I lay on a towel at the foot of Coco's chair. She was wearing her white plastic sunglasses—the ones with lenses the size of salad plates. She was reading *Life* magazine and sipping a Tab—oblivious to the fact that a shark had nearly eaten me.

"Probably just a little ol' sand shark," Beppy said, working on her knitting. "Lots of sand sharks out there."

Why hadn't somebody told us that before now?

"They come in on the tide, chasing the little fish. Nothing to worry about. They won't mess with you kids."

My heart still raced. Adrenaline coursed through my veins. My feet cramped from running in the soft sand.

"Chicken." Joey laughed, standing over me. "Chicken, chicken, chicken," he taunted.

"Shut up," I said, still sucking down air as fast as my nine-year-old lungs would let me. "You ran, too. You're just mad because I beat you."

"Chicken, chicken, chicken."

He was asking for it.

"Shut up," I said again.

"Bwok, bwok, bwok," he cackled.

I'd warned him. That was enough. I got up off the ground and I pounded him until Coco threatened me with a beach-tennis racket.

I felt better. It took a while to calm down.

A few minutes later, I remembered my promise to God.

Oh no, I thought. I'd broken my promise.

I felt bad.

Then I was scared. What did God do to boys who broke promises?

I'd heard stories from the Bible—the old part. I knew what could happen—pestilence, floods, and stuff like that. Sometimes God smote folks. I knew that, too. I could get smitten. What would it be? A lightning bolt? Tripping into a burning bush? Who knew what could happen? Or when?

I shuddered to think about it.

And then I remembered what I'd learned in school about the Crusades and how Christians pillaged and slaughtered and won everything, and how God was on their side because they were skewering infidels—folks who *deserved it.* That's when it occurred to me that it was probably okay to pound a brother if he *deserved it.*

Surely, God knew what I'd intended to promise.

So we, God and I, clarified the deal. I told Him what I'd meant to say—that I wouldn't hit my brothers anymore unless they *deserved it.* And, not to worry, I'd determine whether they *deserved it* because I knew He had better things to do with His time. And then I said "amen" to make it official.

I felt better again.

That first beach trip went so well that we McLeods traveled back to the Georgia coast year after year. Beppy was our beach hostess and

Coco's constant companion. The two of them were inseparable for those two weeks each summer—scrambling eggs together, hauling beach gear, yelling and waving their arms at us kids when we wandered more than knee-deep into the surf, pestering Dad and Dr. Bob to "do something" to get us kids out of harm's way, serving up soggy bologna-and-cheese sandwiches and 7UP from heavy metal coolers, sweeping sand from the kitchen floor of our beach cottage, and tossing up a gigantic green salad each night while the dads burned hot dogs and fat Georgia shrimp on the rusty grill at the edge of the stone patio, outside the screened porch.

After dinner, we kids played hide-and-seek among the sand dunes while the moms cleaned up the kitchen and the dads talked long into the night over glasses of J&B Rare Scotch.

And when the day was done, all eight of us kids—even Betty—lay in our sleeping bags on the screened porch floorboards listening to the crashing surf, chirping crickets, and the croaking of the tiny green frogs clinging to the screen mesh that insulated us from death by mosquito.

Every few minutes, Bart called, "Bep-py, Bep-py." And every few minutes, Beppy or Coco showed up at the porch door to shush us.

As we lay in the dark, warm yellow lamplight stretched from under the kitchen door across the porch floor and onto the sand outside. Adult conversation rose and fell from behind the closed door and a soft breeze full of salty smells wafted in from the darkness beyond the porch.

There was nothing like going to the beach and we owed it all to Coco's abundance of red hair.

25

On the Road

Buffalo, Wyoming

I checked into the Occidental Hotel late, dropped my bag in the room, and talked to Annie for a while before she shooed me off the phone.

"Go on, Sam. You've only got one night in Buffalo. Go get yourself some dinner. And don't be hanging on the bar with any floozies. Or old girlfriends."

"No worries," I said. "I'm going easy on the entertainment tonight. I overdid the macaroni and cheese at Summer's house. You got any idea how many calories there are in macaroni and cheese? I was—"

"No, and I don't want to know," Annie said. "Have you forgotten our little talk? You're supposed to *enjoy* this trip, Sam. Remember? Now, go get a beer and give the weight thing a rest—a long rest."

The Occidental Saloon is high on my list. It's a place that claims Calamity Jane, Butch Cassidy, Buffalo Bill, Teddy Roosevelt, my friend Codger John, and me as former bar decorations. Well, actually, I'm not sure they claim Codger John and me, but we have been there.

I bellied up to the well-worn bar and introduced myself to Katie the Bartender and the couple next to me—Amy and her husband, Roy—who own a forty-thousand-acre ranch near Kaycee.

"Nearly five hundred miles of fence to tend and mend," Amy explained, giving the acreage some scope.

Amy's black cowgirl hat hung from a leather chin strap around her neck and rested on a sun-bleached ponytail that fell in windblown tangles to the middle of her back. Her long-sleeved, dark crimson shirt sported turquoise snaps that matched her eyes. Her Levi's were tight and her boots were dusty with what I preferred to think of as mud. She was a handsome woman and a pleasant conversationalist.

Husband Roy was a long, tall, sandy-haired cowboy who looked to be twice Amy's age and had a limited vocabulary. Without talking to him, you could tell he liked bourbon.

"You two come here often?" I asked.

"Most every night," Amy said. "It's just us and a few hands out at the ranch. They ain't much on gossip. Gets kinda lonely. So, we come into the bar most nights. Right, Roy?"

"Yep," said Roy.

"Everybody we know is here. A right pleasant place," said Amy, admiring her surroundings.

"Came in here about a year ago after fishing with my buddy Codger John," I said. "Been looking forward to a return visit."

"It's a place that'll crawl up under your skin," said Amy. "Right, Roy?"

"Yep."

"So, what're you doing in Buffalo?" Amy asked.

"Just passing through," I said. (It sounded like something a stranger would say.) "I'm on my way to Nashville, Tennessee, to discover the meaning of life."

"Whoa, Sam," Amy said. "Hold your pony right there. That's a tall order and Nashville's a long way from here. I reckon you can drive all that way if you want, but you don't need to go no further."

"How come?" I asked.

"Because Roy knows the meaning of life and he's sitting right here," Amy said. "Right, Roy?"

"Yep."

"So go on now. Tell the man, Roy."

Roy looked up at me, grinned, turned back to his glass, and took another long pull on his bourbon.

"Drinking makes him forgetful," Amy explained. "When he's sober, which ain't too often, he'll tell you life's a full glass of whiskey and a pretty girl in tight jeans. Right, Roy?"

"Yep."

"Well, that's a good thing to know," I said. "I'm feeling lighter already."

"Lighter?" Amy said.

"Yeah. My wife, Annie, told me if I discovered the meaning of life, I'd be able to lose some weight. I can feel the pounds rolling off already."

"Don't appear to be rolling off very fast," Roy said.

Katie the Bartender smiled and put another bourbon under Roy's nose, where he could find it.

"Good for you, Roy! That was darn near a full sentence," Amy said.

This morning, I packed, grabbed a cup of coffee in the hotel lobby, thought about breakfast but figured I'd be better off if I ate one of Annie's apples and a few crackers, and headed out the door.

In the car, I picked up the invitation to the social that lay on the dash. I held it—feeling its grain and the slick black lettering—and read it again, playing old movies in my head.

That's when it hit me. Could Coco be right about Lexi? Was she more than a friend? Is Annie seeing something I'm not? And what about Summer and Marshall? Am I as clueless as they say?

"Surely not," I said aloud, but there wasn't anybody there to hear me.

26

Smitten

There was an old guy in the Occidental Saloon sitting at a table by himself, pretending to sip his drink, but mostly just watching folks come and go. I didn't talk to him, but Katie the Bartender said his name was Cody. Like Amy and Roy, he was there pretty much every night. He looked just like Mr. Birdsong, our elderly neighbor back in Nashville—the fellow who helped us build the Mallorys' tree house and fixed leaky faucets for neighborhood moms. That old man was a real blessing . . .

After Mrs. Birdsong's passing, Mr. Birdsong lived alone in the Hollow's original farmhouse, a 1920s white clapboard box with a dark green roof and matching shutters. Fully leaded paint peeled from the bottoms of sagging gutters and fell into the untamed forsythia surrounding the front porch.

Mrs. Birdsong had furnished the front porch with a green-and-white-striped awning, a massive wrought-iron glider decorated with green plastic-covered cushions, and two white wicker rockers attended by a table just large enough to support a couple of teacups and pie plates. Mr. Birdsong had used a roller brush lashed to a broomstick to paint the cement porch floor a slick brick red.

On summer evenings, Mr. Birdsong rocked himself on the porch glider while he smoked his pipe and surveyed the Hollow through glasses that barely fit over his ears. He grew his ears extra large, he said, because he knew lots of old people who were deaf. He didn't want to be deaf. And he wasn't.

His wardrobe consisted of worn-out flannel shirts and sawdust-covered coveralls. When he wasn't rocking on the front porch, he was out back in his woodworking shop—a converted, single-car garage. He said it was a good thing Mrs. Birdsong was up in heaven, because he'd never hear the end of it if she were there to see what he'd done to her garage.

His shop was cluttered: a stool project here, a bench project there, a lamp spindle on the lathe, a chair hanging by its rockers from rafters above the workbench. Messy piles of lumber everywhere.

In one corner rested an upholstered wing chair that had seen better days, tufts of stuffing blooming from the seat cushion and the armrests. Next to the chair sat a small pine table that Mr. Birdsong had built. And on the table rested the bowl of hard candies Mrs. Birdsong had once kept at their front door.

They weren't ordinary candies. The colorful wrapping gave no hint of the candy inside. No matter how hard we kids puzzled, we couldn't figure out what was inside: cherry? lime? tangerine? pineapple?

Every day after school, we pulled off our school clothes, threw on our play clothes, and hightailed it down to Mr. Birdsong's shop, where we found him hunched over his workbench. No matter what he was doing, he stopped, wiped his bony hands on the oil-stained, paint-splattered rag that lived in his coveralls pocket, seated himself in his threadbare chair, picked up the bowl, and offered us kids a piece of candy—just one piece each.

We hovered around the bowl trying to pick out the right piece. When finally I chose one and started to unwrap it, Mr. Birdsong said, "Now, Sammy, are you sure that's the piece you want?" He planted a tiny seed of doubt that sent me back to the bowl to find a better one. And then he chuckled.

On nice days, we kids ate and ran. Went off to play baseball or Kick-the-Can. But on rainy or cold days, a few of us hung out in Mr. Birdsong's shop and helped him with his projects. Chat glued. Flo sanded. I oiled. Oiling a finely sanded piece of mahogany brought out the wood grain, so we kids could peer deep into the reddish brown spaces between almost-black tree rings, while Mr. Birdsong explained how trees grew and what the tree rings told us about life. And that generally led to a story from Mr. Birdsong's life. Sometimes about Mrs. Birdsong—where she grew up, how they met, when they married, their kids, why Mrs. Birdsong died, whether he missed her, and on and on. Mrs. Birdsong was the only person we'd ever known who'd died.

Flo particularly liked Mr. Birdsong's story about meeting Mrs. Birdsong, or Ruth. She made him tell it over and over again.

They met at a church social in Mr. Birdsong's hometown of Paris, Tennessee, when he was sixteen and she was just fifteen. Ruth's dad was the new minister at the church and brought his family to the social to introduce them around. Mr. Birdsong said when he first saw Ruth, he couldn't take his eyes off of her. Her short, reddish brown hair tied up in a bright red ribbon. Sparkly blue eyes. Dimples when she smiled, and she smiled at everything and everybody with understanding well beyond her years. Mr. Birdsong said he felt like he knew her even though he'd never met her.

Chat and I didn't understand that. It made no sense. But Flo said there was nothing surprising about it, because Mr. Birdsong, without knowing it, was looking at his future bride, and in that special case, things were not supposed to make sense.

Mr. Birdsong smiled, winked at Flo, and speculated that one day we boys would understand. But Flo put on her well-practiced smug look and said she doubted it.

Mr. Birdsong said he was "smitten" the first time he laid eyes on Ruth. I didn't know what "smitten" meant, but got no chance to ask because Flo jumped in and quizzed Mr. Birdsong mercilessly about how Ruth had accomplished the smiting. What was she wearing? What had she said? And how did she look at him?

It was clear that Flo intended to do a little smiting herself someday and wanted to be prepared.

Chat told Flo that she was asking Mr. Birdsong too many questions. But Mr. Birdsong encouraged her to ask away because her questions helped him remember Ruth. He confided that when he was alone in his shop or reading the newspaper while eating his dinner, he often saw Ruth and talked with her. That baffled us, even Flo. How could Ruth talk? She was dead. But Mr. Birdsong told us that for him she wasn't dead, that he often heard her voice and talked with her. And then he said a puzzling thing. He said that one day we'd hear voices, too. He said they'd bring us comfort.

Mr. Birdsong told us it had taken him weeks, after first seeing Ruth, to get up the nerve to talk to her. "What?" I blurted. "She was just a girl." Flo rolled her eyes and put on her smug look again and said something like, "Whenever will you boys grow up?"

Mr. Birdsong smiled and went on saying he'd gotten up his nerve when he saw her talking with another boy after church. Something stirred in him that stiffened his back and walked him right over to Ruth, where he said hello and jabbered a bunch of nonsense. When he finally stopped wagging his tongue, he was so embarrassed by his rambling that he just turned and walked away.

Flo shook her head and said, "Poor Mr. Birdsong," while we boys wondered why he'd been embarrassed.

Just three days later, Mr. Birdsong's mom made him go to the Wednesday night church supper. He dreaded seeing Ruth. He was still so embarrassed about their last encounter that he couldn't bring himself to talk to her. He went straight to the buffet line, hoping to avoid her. He didn't notice when she got in line behind him.

When he turned around and saw her smiling at him, he dropped his napkin-wrapped fork, and then his plate. Potato salad glopped onto one of his shoes. Embarrassment grabbed him again. Again he wanted to get away, but he couldn't leave the mess he'd made.

Ruth said a little succotash on the floor was no big deal. She helped him clean it up and asked him if he'd sit with her when he got another plate of food.

After shoveling some banana pudding onto the edge of his new plate, he looked up to find Ruth waiting patiently for him. She sat on a gray metal fold-up chair in the corner of the room, her plate in her lap, another chair next to her. A Dixie cup full of iced tea rested on the empty chair. She picked it up as he headed her way.

As if they'd known each other forever, Ruth started right in talking about moving to a new town and how shy she was and how difficult it was to talk to new people. She went on to say that she felt like he could understand and that talking with him—even though he wasn't talking at all—was easier because he understood.

After that night, Mr. Birdsong said, he and Ruth were inseparable.

"Until she died," Chat said.

Mr. Birdsong said nothing more. He turned back to his workbench, found a piece of fine sandpaper, and rubbed it over the lamp spindle as the lathe turned. Chat went back to gluing, Flo went back to sanding, and I went back to oiling. Somehow we knew that the talk was over, at least for a while.

■   ■   ■

And then one day when we kids arrived at Mr. Birdsong's shop to get a piece of candy, we found the door shut. Through a window, we could see that the lights were off. We stood there for the longest time wondering what had happened.

Then a woman's voice called from the back door of Mr. Birdsong's house. It was his daughter, Lindsey. She said Mr. Birdsong had fallen in the kitchen and broken his hip. The doctors put a cast on his leg from his waist to his toes and ordered him to bed. He wanted us to come up to his room; he had the candy bowl in his room.

We'd never been upstairs in Mr. Birdsong's house. It had a narrow, dark stairway with an oak handrail. Mr. Birdsong lay in his bed under a quilt covered in pink pigs with green apples in their mouths. The shades were pulled. The room smelled of rubbing alcohol. A plastic tube ran into Mr. Birdsong's nose. He couldn't talk above a whisper but asked Lindsey to get the bowl, which she placed on the bed beside him. He motioned for us to come close.

While we worried over the candy in the bowl, Mr. Birdsong said he was going up to heaven to be with Mrs. Birdsong. He said the doctors couldn't fix his leg and he wasn't the kind to put up with a wheelchair. Lindsey's eyes leaked a few tears. She wiped them away with the back of her hand.

Mr. Birdsong said he wasn't ever going to forget us kids. He'd be looking down from heaven to see how we were doing and he'd talk to us if we asked him to. He wanted us to take the bowl and find a good place for it where we could get a piece of candy each afternoon. He'd be watching, he said.

A few days later, Mr. Birdsong died. From the front yard, we watched the comings and goings at his house. His family arrived in dribs and drabs. And then, except for Lindsey, they all disappeared. The next week, an orange moving van pulled up in front of the house and took everything away.

For some time, the bowl found a home on the green-painted chest next to the milk dispenser in our breakfast room. Visiting kids grabbed the occasional piece of candy, but it wasn't the same. Gradually the bowl fell into disuse and one day it was gone.

It resurfaced a couple of years ago. Annie found it in a storage box in the basement and asked me if I knew anything about it.

I did, but couldn't explain how I'd ended up with it. Annie loved the story.

The bowl now sits on a corner of my desk, full of loose change, old keys, orphaned buttons, and a bunch of other stuff. And every time I notice it, I see Mr. Birdsong. Sometimes I hear his voice.

27

Getting Some Education

Before we chose our piece of hard candy each afternoon, we had to survive an entire day of school. Easier said than done . . .

H. G. Hill Elementary School was a low-slung, redbrick, U-shaped af-fair with louvered classroom windows. In 1956, our little institution of elementary edification was so overrun with baby boomers that tempo-rary classrooms (double-wide trailers) were rolled into place on a grassy strip of land behind the school. Those temporary rooms, or "portables" as we called them, would be there for the next twenty years.

From Mrs. Galloway's first-grade classroom, I had an unobstructed view of the playground, a bare dirt area the size of a Pee Wee Baseball diamond. One aging steel-barred jungle gym (harvested from another playground somewhere) stood alone in the middle of the playground, its feet sunk into cement beneath the hard-baked clay.

I sat at a left-handed desk in the back corner of the room, and Lexi sat next to me at a right-handed desk. As the crow flies, we were as far from the teacher as we could get. With some thirty kids and just one teacher crammed into our little room, there were plenty of bad actors between Mrs. Galloway and me. While I was not the least of her worries, I was not on her most-wanted list. So, I was free to spend my time as I pleased: looking out the window or trapping black flies in my cigar box.

School rules required each first grader to have a cigar box full of school supplies: fat pencils, safety scissors, a gum eraser that crumbled better than it erased, a six-inch ruler, Elmer's glue, and a box of Crayola crayons (the one with sixteen crayons in it, not the big box). So, Coco took me to West Meade Pharmacy, where old Doc Cheek dispensed prescription drugs and cheap cigars. At the back of the pharmacy, he had a storeroom full of empty cigar boxes, and he encouraged me to rummage around in there for as long as I wanted while Coco gathered school supplies and other stuff.

My cigar box was unadorned. Lexi decorated hers with pink construction paper and silver sprinkles that spelled out "School Supplies," a rare bit of evidence that Lexi had girly leanings.

I liked to empty my cigar box and trap unwary flies. I put a dab of Elmer's glue in the bottom of the box, propped the lid open with a pencil stub, sat back, and waited patiently. Pretty soon a hapless fly would happen by and dive into the Elmer's, the ham biscuit of the housefly world. Pretty soon every kid in the back row became a trapper.

Lexi learned how to catch a fly and pull just one wing off so it'd spin helplessly in the bottom of her cigar box while she reset her trap to catch more. That practice quickly spread among us trappers. I once had seven flies spinning in the bottom of my cigar box, but that was nowhere near the record. Albert Hale boasted twelve spinners at one time, a record that stands to this day (as far as I know).

Gazing out the window was my second favorite thing to do in first grade. I kept one ear on Mrs. Galloway and one ear on the playground. At some point most every day, a kid plunged from the top of the jungle gym, or got whacked with a baseball bat, or suffered serious injury during a game of Smear-the-Man-with-the-Ball. Ear-piercing wails were reliable indicators of in-process carnage and suggested that looking out the window would be time well spent.

One day a big kid—a fourth grader, I think—was high-wire-walking the top of the jungle gym when another big kid shook it enough to send the high-wire act off course. The daredevil lost his balance and plummeted headfirst to the ground.

Blood flowed. The kid screamed like a banshee and attracted the attention of our entire class, causing a rush to the windows. Mrs. Galloway threatened and cajoled for a bit, but finally gave in to our collective rubbernecking.

The screaming stopped suddenly. The big kid lay still in the red dirt. Miss Watson, one of the fourth-grade teachers, ran from the playground to the back door of our school while Miss Walker and about sixty bug-eyed kids hovered over the injured boy.

Pretty soon Miss Watson, Mrs. Hearn, the principal, and Mrs. Honesty, the school nurse ran onto the playground with towels and covered the victim head to toe. An ambulance arrived, then a fire truck, sirens blaring.

It was difficult to see over the heads of the kids who'd rushed the classroom windows, so we last-row kids stood in our seats to get a better view. And that's when Tommy Wheelright toppled from his desk chair into a louvered-window frame and knocked out a bunch of his teeth. Blood oozed from his mouth and pooled up under his head as he lay moaning on the floor.

While the girls near him shrieked, Mrs. Galloway held a wet rag to Tommy's mouth. When he quit shaking, Mrs. Galloway walked him down the hall to the infirmary, leaving the rest of us to choose between watching the action on the playground and looking for Tommy's teeth.

It was one of the very best first-grade days we ever had.

The big kid lived, but suffered a broken leg and a minor concussion. He came back to school sporting a cast on his leg, wooden crutches, a heavily bandaged head, and a new book bag hung over one shoulder. He was a hero of sorts.

Tommy Wheelright lost five teeth. Fortunately they were all baby teeth, so he walked around toothless for a year or so until his permanent teeth showed up. He never achieved hero status.

One gorgeous spring day, I was looking out the window, minding my own business, when I heard my name called. "Sammy McLeod," Mrs. Galloway said, "it's your day. Come on up here for show-and-tell."

Oh no. I didn't have anything to share. I'd forgotten that it was my show-and-tell day. My bowels churned.

Why didn't I simply admit that I'd forgotten? Mrs. Galloway tolerated occasional forgetfulness. I could have avoided a big mistake.

Instead I found myself walking to the front of the classroom not knowing what I'd do when I got there. I stood next to Mrs. Galloway's desk and faced my classmates, all thirty of them. I looked at them for a very long time. I sucked down oxygen. And then I started telling a story about driving out to the country on Sunday, just the day before, to a farmhouse up on top of a hill, surrounded by giant sycamore trees, looking down on acres of cotton, where a nice man, one of my dad's patients, raised yellow retriever puppies. The nice man led my brothers and me to Rosie and her new litter. My dad said I was old enough to have a dog of my own and told my brothers and me to pick one out to take home. And we did.

My puppy, Bud, had big brown eyes, large floppy ears, and huge paws. He loved chewing on fingers and ratty tennis balls. My brothers and I played with Bud that afternoon until Bud fell down in the grass, rolled over on his back, and went to sleep.

After dinner, my mom and I put down some newspaper in the guest bathroom on the tile floor, where a little puppy mess would be easy to clean up. We turned out the lights and left Bud in there all alone. He whimpered pitifully well into the night. Even though my mom had forbidden it, I snuck out of my room and down the hall to rescue him. I carried him back to my bed, where he curled up beside me with his cold nose in my armpit. Bud and I slept all night like that.

My classmates stared at me wide-eyed, their mouths agape. They loved my story. I loved telling it. And oh, how I loved the feeling that all of a sudden I was somebody. I was no longer little Sammy McLeod who sat in the last row of left-handed desks. Nope, now I was Sammy McLeod, puppy owner and a popular guy. And I really, really liked that.

There was only one small problem: the story was a complete fabrication, what Annie would call a big lie.

That afternoon when school let out, adoring classmates surrounded me and begged me to invite them over to play with Bud. It was Mrs. Mallory's day to drive car pool. Zeke, Lexi, and Chat were already in the car whooping and hollering to her that she should take me home first so they could see Sammy's new puppy, Bud. Mrs. Mallory crinkled her brow and narrowed her eyes. She said she hadn't heard about a new puppy. So I told her my story about picking Bud up, just the day before, which was why she hadn't heard about our new puppy yet.

We drove down the Big Road while I retold my story, adding interesting little details here and there. By the time we arrived at my house, we were one excited bunch of kids. I'd started to believe the story myself, so it wasn't until we turned into the driveway that I recognized an upcoming problem. I piped up, saying how sorry I was.

I'd forgotten that my mom was taking Bud to the vet to get his puppy shots. He wouldn't be home when we got up to the house.

We pulled up to the back door, where Lexi spied my mom's car and screeched with delight. Now we'd be able to see Bud.

I said no, no, no, I'd forgotten to tell them that Mom was having some trouble with the Toad and was afraid to drive it, so Mrs. Whitley had offered to take her and Bud to the veterinarian. Bud wasn't home.

I jumped out of the car, promising that they'd see Bud the next morning when the car pool came to pick me up. I ran to the back door and disappeared into the house.

The next morning arrived. I dreaded school. Keeping my story straight required a lot of thinking. My brain was starting to hurt. It was Mrs. Witherspoon's driving day. When she pulled up at our back door, I bolted from the house and jumped into her car before the other kids could pile out and start asking a bunch of tough questions about Bud. I explained that my dad had taken Bud on a hike in the hills, and suggested that we drive on to school. We'd see Bud after school when Mrs. Witherspoon picked us up.

Mrs. Witherspoon pulled out of our driveway but asked a sack-load of questions about why my dad would take an eight-week-old puppy on a hike in the hills when she suspected that he'd never set foot in those hills himself. They were good questions.

That afternoon Miss Field, the principal's secretary, came to Mrs. Galloway's room, interrupted class, and whispered to Mrs. Galloway about something. My bowels started churning again.

Sure enough, Mrs. Galloway called out my name and asked me to come with her. She explained to the class that Miss Field was going to stand in for her while she and I went for a little walk to the principal's office.

I did not take that as a good sign.

When Mrs. Galloway and I arrived at Mrs. Hearn's office, there were Coco, Mrs. Witherspoon, Mrs. Mallory, my dad, and, of course, Mrs. Hearn—all waiting to greet me. There were so many folks in there that Mrs. Galloway and my dad had to bring in a couple of extra chairs.

And then we all had a too-long conversation about Bud, and making up stories, and telling the truth, and how important that was, and how there'd likely be some consequences to deal with when I got home that afternoon. Which there were.

I learned an important lesson that day: Never tell a lie unless you've thought it all the way through.

28

Dr. Pritchard

Bloody accidents in the neighborhood. Bloody accidents on the playground. Bloody accidents in the church parking lot. Thank goodness for Dr. Pritchard . . .

The fifties were good to Dr. Arthur Willis Pritchard.

A highly regarded surgeon, he repaired thousands of broken femurs, mended countless broken hearts, and removed an epidemic of dyspeptic gallbladders.

He was a giant of a man, bigger than any Jolley I knew. He smoked bad cigars and smelled like the inside of a chimney. When he tilted his big head to get a better look at tibia fragments protruding from a kid's shin, his jowls flapped against his white coat and his mouse-brown bouffant hairpiece slid around on his head like a bearskin on skates. He claimed his hairpiece was stuck to his head tighter than a tick on a coonhound, but he wore a green-mesh hairnet during surgery to contain his extravagant hairdo and make sure it didn't end up on the wrong side of a surgical scar. The few folks who saw him without his toupee said he reminded them of Alfred Hitchcock.

During the summer of '58, the Pritchard family moved into a three-story, white-columned mansion in the city of Belle Meade, a swanky suburb of Nashville that pretended to be a long way from pawnshops full of guitars just a few blocks up the street. Ancient oaks and lush well-groomed grounds surrounded the manor house. An army of groundskeepers worked the place over from dawn to dusk, paying special attention to the removal of oil stains on the cobblestone drive. A fellow named Marvin answered the door while his wife, Simone, kept the Pritchards and their guests hydrated and caffeinated with Lipton iced tea.

Mrs. Pritchard, a former high school homecoming queen and head cheerleader, married well, taking on a name that fit her to a pink-marble pedestal. She gave the term *trophy wife* new life as she strutted, tittered, and flitted about, barking high-pitched commands around the manor like she was born to it.

Unfortunately, the years beyond high school had not been kind to Mrs. Pritchard, a situation made worse by the fact that she didn't know it. Under the care of Franco, Nashville's most-sought-after hairdresser, Mrs. Pritchard's dirty-brown locks were replaced with a flamingo-pink nest that looked like it belonged in the bowl of a cotton-candy machine. Without any care at all, her firm, melon-size breasts sagged into an ample bosom and Bermuda shorts did little to hide dimpled thighs. Short, fat toes—toenails painted pink to match her hair—gripped the soles of her summer flats in such a way as to suggest that they were hanging on for dear life.

When she wasn't ordering underlings about or fawning over important guests, Mrs. Pritchard bragged about her children and pressed them for more achievements to add to her arsenal. As a consequence, the eight Pritchard children attended private schools and took piano lessons. They played on their high school golf teams, tennis teams, and swim teams, and were so skilled in these country-club sports that the least athletic among them were stars.

The family vacationed in Europe for several weeks each summer. When they weren't vacationing, they lounged around the pool and dined on fancy white linens at the Belle Meade Country Club.

On Sunday afternoons, Pritchard aunts, uncles, and cousins gathered at the mansion for croquet. Between exhausting matches, they drank Simone's sun tea and nibbled on sweet biscuits, while Marvin swept leaves from the field of play and replaced the occasional divot.

And they owed it all to us.

As you've gathered by now, about once a week, one of us neighborhood kids fell out of a tree, or over a cliff, or into a machine of some sort and severed a body part or punctured a vital organ so badly that stitches were required. Following an injury that produced copious bleeding or a concussion of hallucinogenic proportions, we kids summoned the nearest mom to preside over the grisly scene. She'd issue the orders: "Sammy, you run home and call Dr. Pritchard's office. Tell Miss Trudy that Chat has cracked his skull wide open and his brains are falling out. Tell her I'm scooping them up now and will meet Dr. Pritchard at the emergency room in twenty minutes."

"Lexi, you run up to the Whitleys' house and get Mrs. Whitley to give you four or five bath towels, not her good ones. Tell her we don't need the Lysol."

"Wiener, you help me get Chat out of this ditch and up to the road."

"Carrot Top, you and Wiener sit here with Chat until I get the car."

And that's the way it went until the rescuing mom zoomed off to

the hospital with Chat and his brains wrapped in ratty towels. Wide-
eyed kids and a pool of blood left in their wake.

Miss Trudy answered the good doctor's phone. Near as we could
tell, she never took a lunch break or a day off or went to church. She
knew our voices and called us by name. After one of us delivered the
message about the latest injury, Trudy said, "Alrighty," and hung up.
She did not waste time. Dr. Pritchard was on the case.

Dr. Pritchard met the injured at Vanderbilt Hospital Emergency Room. There were other good hospitals in Nashville, but Dr.
Pritchard's office was just a few blocks from Vanderbilt. When anybody
in our neighborhood said "emergency room," she meant Vanderbilt.

I don't know how Dr. Pritchard made it there ahead of us every
time, but he did. Coco said he'd run out of surgery, right in the middle of removing somebody's heart, to take care of a neighborhood kid.
The heart surgery patient would have to wait.

Dr. Pritchard knew who buttered his bread.

We loved Dr. Pritchard even though our experience with him was
mostly unpleasant. It may have had something to do with the Her-
shey Kisses he pulled from his pocket as he sent us home, or the
gigantic box of fireworks he delivered to our neighborhood every
Christmas for our New Year's Eve celebration.

We couldn't wait until December 31. Most every night between
Christmas and New Year's, neighborhood kids and their dads congre-
gated in our backyard. We tossed firecrackers at each other, launched
bottle rockets at the dogs, and shot off Big Boomers while Dr.
Pritchard sat patiently by his phone.

Occasionally, one of us suffered a minor injury, a slight burn from
grabbing the wrong end of a sparkler, or a gunpowder-blackened finger
from firecracker tossing. These little inconveniences stopped the show
for a few minutes while my dad (the doctor) examined the injury under
a flashlight and uttered something soothing like "You'll live."

The carnage resumed.

Coco did not care for fireworks. She spent her time between meals pleading with my dad to "use the single grain of sense God gave you" and "stop the madness."

It didn't work.

Dad said he could deal with an emergency if there were one, but emergencies were unlikely because we were careful. He cited as evidence the fact that nobody had died or lost a limb yet. He said he'd reconsider if somebody expired or lost an appendage.

That didn't make Coco feel any better. She threw up her hands and gazed skyward for assistance. None was forthcoming. God took Dad's side.

Having gotten nowhere with Dad or God, Coco turned on us boys and tried to scare us, reading aloud from the newspaper about children maimed for life by fireworks.

That didn't work, either.

So she prayed aloud for our deliverance and that seemed to work just fine.

The holidays were tough on Coco.

Over the years, Dr. Pritchard removed four sets of McLeod tonsils, my appendix, rock fragments from the top of Harry's head, a splinter the size of a toothpick from the corner of Joey's eye, and a Hog's Feather steel-tipped competition dart from Mikey's left wrist.

Joey held the record for emergency-room visits in the "head-injuries" category, making three trips to get his head stitched up. Ricky and Harry both made that trip twice. Mikey did the head-injury trip once, and I dodged it altogether. Head injuries were the worst.

Harry held the McLeod family record in the "overall" category, having endured head injuries, severed body parts, noncranial lacerations, and unfortunate swallowings. His two head-injury trips were from falling off the roof into the woodpile and bonking his head on the handlebar of his bike after launching himself off the Mallorys' trampoline. He survived four noncranial lacerations, and one unfortunate swallowing of a plastic army man—luckily just an infantryman without a bayoneted rifle. There were no stitches for the swallowing, but Harry had to drink a pint-size bottle of pink stuff, the emergency-room equivalent of triple-strength Ex-Lax, before Dr. Pritchard let him go home.

Even so, none of us McLeods, or other neighborhood kids for that matter, came anywhere close to the record set by Carrot Top Whitley. In the first decade of his miraculous life, he went to the emergency room a total of nineteen times. He was one of Dr. Pritchard favorites, a kid who suffered near-death experiences with alarming regularity but never crossed the line. Dad figured Carrot Top had singlehandedly delivered the Pritchards their new tennis court with the fancy all-weather surface.

According to Coco, had Dr. Pritchard not been there to save our young lives, only Bobby Whitley and Honey Bee Littlejohn would have survived childhood in the Hollow.

While we threw firecrackers at each other and fired bottle rockets at the dogs, Coco busied herself with making pickled shrimp for her annual New Year's Eve party. She said the shrimp were for the guests and warned us boys not to pilfer any of them. But just before the party, she always gave us each one shrimp and promised that there'd be leftovers for us if we behaved ourselves.

Well, one year there were no leftovers and we learned a valuable lesson. From that day forward, every time Coco put on her New Year's party, we showed up for our preparty shrimp but then hovered around the bowl along with the guests, letting the ladies pinch our cheeks while they said, "I do declare, you boys have grown a foot since last year." We shook hands with the men and smiled while everybody talked about how handsome we were.

And we accepted the shrimp offered by our many admirers.

Coco's Pickled Shrimp

Serves 20 as an appetizer

Ingredients

For the shrimp:

2½ pounds large fresh Atlantic coast or Gulf shrimp

½ cup celery tops

¼ cup pickling spices

3 teaspoons kosher salt

2 medium onions, sliced into thin rings

7 bay leaves (a lucky number)

For the marinade:

¾ cup white vinegar

1½ cups vegetable oil

2½ tablespoons capers

2½ teaspoons celery seed

1½ teaspoons kosher salt

¼ teaspoon hot sauce (preferably, Tabasco)

AND a box of multicolored toothpicks for serving

PLACE the shrimp, celery tops, pickling spices, and salt in a large pot of boiling water and cook the shrimp until they are just cooked through, about three minutes. Drain the shrimp in a colander, rinse under cold running water until cool to the touch, remove shells and tails, and devein.

PLACE a layer of onions in the bottom of a large, fancy, glass bowl. Then a layer of shrimp. Then a layer of onions, etc. Continue layering until you've used up all the shrimp and onions. Insert the bay leaves to distribute them evenly among the shrimp.

COMBINE the marinade ingredients and stir well. Pour the marinade over the shrimp. Cover the bowl and chill in the refrigerator for a full day before serving, tossing a couple of times each day to coat the shrimp with the marinade.

THIS is a real crowd-pleaser.

29

On the Road
Columbia, Missouri

I limped into Columbia, weary of driving.

Alice, Charlie, Millie, and Ted were already sitting around the picnic table on the screened porch—ribs on the grill, salad in a large wooden bowl on the table, and apple pie in the oven. The place smelled edible.

Three of these good people are doctors and the fourth is a nutritional counselor. You'd expect them to walk the healthy-diet talk, wouldn't you?

"Do you guys have any idea what we're getting ready to do to ourselves?" I asked, climbing over a picnic bench and sitting down. "I met this guy Rudy day before yesterday when I stopped in Big Timber . . ."

I told them all about counting calories at Cole Drugs and the un-savory truth about ribs and apple pie with Cheddar cheese.

"And here we are having ribs and apple pie and you're all doctors. You people are hypocrites."

"I'm giving up hypocrisy first thing tomorrow morning," Dr. Char-lie said, toting a platter piled high in succulent pork, slathered with secret-recipe sauce thick as jam.

For the next several hours, we feasted on Charlie's ribs, choked down some lettuce, and lingered over Alice's homemade apple pie with Cheddar cheese—a stunner of a pie. We caught up on fam-ily news, swapped stories about reunions and old flames, speculated about the benefits of pork fat, wallowed in the history of Alice's apple pie, and drank a beer or two. It was a wonderful night—one I'll never forget.

And then, this morning as I was leaving . . .

"Sam," Charlie said. "The older I get, the more old folks I doctor, the more I think life's all about balance. We're both on the heavier end of the scale, so we've got to stay active. And maybe salad's a good choice now and again. But we need to be enjoying ourselves, too—like those ribs, Alice's pie, that social you're going to, and the company of old girlfriends. Unless your weight is messing with your health, I wouldn't worry over it. The worry is probably hurting more than the pounds. I wish I were going to see an old girlfriend."

Alice kicked Charlie and gave me a hug. "You leave those old girlfriends alone, Sam McLeod. You've got a good one. Tell Annie we enjoyed your visit and you bring her with you next time, you hear?"

"I will," I said. "Thanks for everything, including the lecture. I needed it."

I settled into my all-too-familiar seat behind the wheel—feeling a little better about things—and rolled down the windows.

The Grateful Dead were playing on the radio. I turned up the volume, put on my sunglasses, checked my good looks in the rearview mirror, repeated the word *balance*, waved good-bye, and headed for Jackson, Tennessee.

> *Truckin',*
> *I'm a-goin' home.*
> *Whoa whoa, baby,*
> *Back where I belong . . .*

30

Here Comes the Judge

I was driving too fast as I crossed the Mississippi River and touched down in the land of my upbringing. Don't want to do time in a Tennessee jail, I thought . . . like I almost did once . . . long, long ago . . .

I awoke and lay in my bed, listening for everyday noises—cars passing along the Big Road, the clank of pots and pans, the flush of a toilet—but I heard nothing. Except for the ticking of Little Ben on the dresser, the world was awfully quiet.

Joey hurdled the foot of his bunk, yanked the window shade, and let go. It whacked the window frame above his head while we peered into the whiteness. A scattering of crystals drifted out of the pearl-gray sky.

Buzzed on hope, we sprinted to the kitchen. Glistening strips of crisp bacon were piled high on a folded grocery bag, oiling the brown paper. White bread slices stood in the toaster. The kitchen smelled of perking coffee. A Pyrex bowl at the edge of the stove was full of fork-whipped eggs. Cheese grits spluttered in a cast-iron pot on the back burner. Krispy Kreme donuts were on the table.

Coco stood at the sink sectioning grapefruit halves.

Dad sat at the table, his shirt collar unbuttoned and tieless, sipping coffee, scanning last night's newspaper. The morning paper hadn't been delivered.

That cinched it: no school.

Snow was so predictable back in the good ol' days that we each had a snowsuit, an awkward, heavily padded, navy-blue coverall. We labored through the suiting-up process. With Coco's help we pulled on layer after layer: pajama bottoms with badly worn knees and torn stocking feet, long-sleeved turtlenecked shirts so ketchup-stained that they were no longer acceptable school wear, heavy wool sweaters that made us itch just looking at them, several pairs of equally itchy wool socks, and grass-stained blue jeans that wouldn't buckle up over all those layers. Then and only then did Coco shove us into our snowsuits, pulling and stretching where necessary to help those suits carry us frostbite-free through another winter.

Next the boots—black rubber galoshes that offered little insulation but came with a mangle of metal clips. Coco went boy by boy, shoving our bulky socked feet into them and buckling them after making the necessary adjustments.

We wore mittens, not gloves. I'm still embarrassed about it. Adding insult to injury, Coco covered our mittens in plastic sandwich bags and rubber-banded them around our wrists like tourniquets, apparently unaware that the loss of blood flow to our fingertips encouraged the frostbite she was trying so hard to avoid. None of our friends wore mittens or sandwich bags. We were the laughingstock of the neighborhood.

Overheated, unable to bend enough to grab the sled towrope, and red-faced with embarrassment, we trudged into the backyard, where we sledded a barely perceptible rise while all the other kids (except Bobby Whitley) sledded the Course at the Bradley Smiths' and had what was reported to be the time of their short lives.

Coco wasn't convinced that we were capable of getting to the Bradley Smiths' and back in one piece. According to her, I was not yet old enough to sled the Course. Lexi, who was six like me *and* a girl, went by herself. Coco didn't care. I was confined along with my brothers to the "bunny slope" in our backyard—boring, just the way Coco liked it.

It was not until I turned seven that Coco relented and allowed me to roam up the Hollow to the edge of the world as I knew it.

On snow days, I inhaled a couple of Krispy Kreme donuts, bolted down a plate of scrambled eggs, bacon, several pieces of Wonder bread toast slathered in butter and grape jelly, finished my milk, struggled into my snowsuit, thumbed my nose at my brothers, and headed up valley. That was the easy part. Climbing the Course from the Big Road was torture.

There was only one Course rule: No sledding into the Big Road. Any kid caught sledding into the road lost sledding privileges for the rest of the winter, a fate worse than death. It was better to go off the driveway bridge into Moccasin Creek and take your chances on a trip to Dr. Pritchard. Best was a deft right-hand turn, just before the bridge, into the willows that lined the creek. They were pretty good at stopping an out-of-control sled without killing the driver.

We normally sledded until our toes throbbed and then went numb. But occasionally, sledding was cut short by an injury to one of our group requiring Mrs. Bradley Smith or another mom to haul one of us to the emergency room. And that is what happened late on a Tuesday morning in February of 1958.

■   ■   ■

Over time, a number of sledding records were established on the Course: longest ride, fastest ride, longest ride sledding flat on your belly, longest ride sledding in a seated position, longest ride sledding two-man (a rider on your back), fastest ride on the short sled with the newly polished runners from the garage door to the creek, seated backward, blindfolded, with one hand on the guide bar and the other behind the back.

Seeking a new record on the short sled, Possum hit the stone wall in Curve Three, rolled the sled onto its side, and kept sliding. Unable to control his speed, direction, or anything else, he slid halfway across the driveway bridge headed for the Big Road before taking the decision to abandon ship and launch himself headfirst into Moccasin Creek.

It did not take long for Junior, Zeke, Lexi, and me to gather on the bridge looking down at Possum, who had broken through the ice at the edge of the creek and lay flat on his back, bleeding from a gash on his head, thick red blood spreading over the ice.

At first we thought Possum was playing dead. (He came by his nickname honestly.) But pretty soon we figured he wasn't.

Junior yelled up the hill, "Chat, go get my mom. Tell her Possum is lying in the creek not playing dead."

Chat, slip-sliding down the Course to see what had happened, hollered back, "You go tell her. She's your mom and besides I haven't seen the blood yet."

"*Somebody* get Mrs. Bradley Smith," Lexi shrieked. "Possum might really be dead."

And Chat, arriving on the scene, said, "If he's dead, there's no reason to hurry."

That's the way it went until Possum opened his eyes, moaned like he meant it, and begged us to get his mom because he couldn't move his leg. Then he touched the side of his head, took one look at his blood-covered hand, moaned again, and passed out.

Junior ran up the hill to get his mom.

Mrs. Bradley Smith, puffing on a Superslim, skated down the Course in her pink bedroom slippers with the Mickey Mouse ears on them. She was wearing a matching pink terry-cloth bathrobe under her full-length mink coat and had a red scarf tied over a black hairnet. She'd misplaced her glasses, so she squinted like Mr. Magoo.

Coco drove slowly up the Big Road in the Tadpole. Mrs. Bradley Smith had already called her, saying she couldn't get her car down the driveway and a trip to Dr. Pritchard was likely required.

After Coco and Mrs. Bradley Smith loaded Possum into the Tadpole, where he lay whimpering, and after Mrs. Bradley Smith grabbed Junior by the collar and told him he was going to the emergency room with them whether he wanted to or not, and after Coco sent Chat home to call Miss Trudy at Dr. Pritchard's office and let her know they were headed to the emergency room with Possum, I headed home to recover the feeling in my toes.

Coco arrived home about lunchtime and reported that Possum had a bad headache and a big bandage, but no broken bones. He'd have to stay inside for a few days, but would be fine. She fixed us toasted cheese and onion sandwiches, chips, and hot chocolate before helping us back into our snowsuits and sending us outside.

I saw Chat piling up snow at the foot of his driveway. He had a couple of bread pans. He said he was going to make snow bricks and build a fort at the Big Curve in the Big Road.

By dusk, we'd constructed a fully functional igloo. We left a hole in the roof to let the smoke out even though we had no fire. And that is where we left it, Chat saying I should come down early the next morning to help him finish up.

Bright and early the next day, Chat and I excavated a pit just inside the entrance to our fort to hold the snowballs we'd use to fend off invaders. We'd never had any invaders in the Hollow near as I could remember, but if any came calling, we'd be ready. By lunchtime, we'd manufactured enough snowballs to fill the pit and figured it was time to take up our posts.

It being lunchtime, there weren't any other kids out. My brothers were probably drinking hot chocolate and eating tuna salad sandwiches. Mrs. Witherspoon hollered for Chat to come in for lunch. My stomach grumbled. But Chat told me to stay with the fort until he got back. What if invaders showed up and there was nobody to defend the neighborhood? I had to admit he had a point and, like I said, I did what older kids told me to do.

So, I hung out in the igloo, bored out of my gourd. I watched water drops splat on an ice brick left over from the construction. I rearranged the snowballs a few times. I lay on my back, noticing how blue light crept in around the edges of the snow bricks. I listened to my stomach and wished Chat would get back so I could go home for lunch.

The Hollow was dead quiet except for a rumbling noise way up valley, a rumbling that came and went on a stiff breeze for a while and then came steady and grew louder. Invaders!

A whale of a Cadillac came into view beyond the Bradley Smiths' and lumbered toward me, sporting black tail fins, sliding this way and that on the icy road. It slowed as it approached the Big Curve. I crouched down inside the fort, grabbed two softball-size snowballs, and waited.

As the Cadillac crawled through the Big Curve, I scrambled out of the fort and let those snowballs fly, one of 'em landing a direct hit on the windshield and the other landing harmlessly in the road. I never could throw right-handed.

The massive machine stopped. Judge Berkeley stared at me from the backseat.

We neighborhood kids were scared to death of Judge Berkeley. He lived way up valley near the Turner Smiths and had a reputation for meanness and miserly ways. When Possum and Junior went to the judge's house on Halloween once, the judge's driver, Spitz, handed them a few pieces of candy corn while the judge stood in the doorway glaring at them. That was the last time they went. The place was too scary for words.

I had only seen Judge Berkeley once myself when Spitz cut his arm on a garage door and the judge drove him to our place so my dad could have a look at it, hoping he wouldn't have to go to Dr. Pritchard.

Spitz left the big Caddy idling in the middle of the Big Road and came over to the fort, where I stood frozen like an ice sculpture. He recognized me as one of the McLeod boys and asked which one I was.

I mumbled, "Sammy."

Spitz said the judge wanted him to look the car over for damage and would probably be in touch with Coco. I nodded. And they drove off.

And I ran home. My stomach hurt.

I couldn't eat any lunch. In the Little Den, my brothers were cobbling together a tent city out of worn blankets and arguing over some lumpy, badly stained pillows. I found a corner in the tent and covered my head with a pillowcase. The sick feeling was not going away.

The phone rang. I couldn't make out what Coco was saying but it sounded serious.

My stomach felt worse.

The next thing I knew, Coco was at the Little Den door calling me out where she could see me. She wanted to know what had happened down at the Witherspoons' with Judge Berkeley and Spitz. I told her about the fort and the snowballs and invaders and hitting the judge's car with one snowball . . . sorta . . . and missing altogether with the other one . . . and that it would never happen again I promised . . . and so on and so forth.

She said she thought that was probably right, because the judge was sending Spitz to pick me up and take me to jail.

My stomach turned somersaults.

I was speechless; even my brothers were speechless.

Coco allowed the news to sink in and said we'd have to pack up some of my clothes because I might be in jail awhile. My brothers came back to life: Would the guards feed Sammy in jail? Would he be able to order what he wanted? Did they serve fish sticks? What about Tater Tots? Would they make Sammy eat peas? Did prisoners get dessert? Would he be in a cell by himself? Or with other convicts? What if Sammy was locked up with a murderer? Did murderers murder folks in jail? Would Coco take them to see Sammy in jail? Could we make him a cake with a kitchen knife in it?

They talked about me like I was already gone.

Once my bag was packed, I lay on the sofa in the Little Den in a fetal position and felt my stomach churning. Brothers bounced off the walls around me. Joey wanted me to remember every part of going to jail so I could tell them about it, if I ever got out. Then Ricky bolted from the window where he'd been watching for the big black Cadillac, screaming that Spitz was headed up the driveway and, whoopee, Sammy was going to jail.

The next thing I remember hearing was Judge Berkeley's voice at the Little Den door, where he was talking to Coco. I hadn't expected the judge. The whole thing was getting worse by the second. Coco came and fetched me and my bag to the door, where I stood looking at the judge. He asked if I was ready to go to jail and I said I was. Harry kept interrupting, asking if the jail had fish sticks and Tater Tots. But the judge was not easily distracted.

He wanted to know how many times I'd been to jail. I said none. He asked me if I was sorry for pitching the snowball at his car. I said yes sir, I was. He asked if I knew that throwing snowballs at a car could scare a driver so badly he'd run into the ditch, or worse, the creek? And I said I hadn't thought about that, but was still sorry.

He said he'd heard he had a reputation among the neighborhood kids as a mean and miserly old man. Joey piped up and said that was correct on account of just giving candy corn for Halloween. While Coco was begging Joey to hold his tongue, Harry said that kids were getting way more than candy corn at most houses. Ricky said he liked Three Musketeers bars, the regular-size ones, not the little ones they made for Halloween. Mikey nodded. Coco tried to shush Ricky, but before she could, the judge asked what other kinds of candy Spitz should buy. He said he didn't have any kids and didn't know what was expected.

Well, there it went. My brothers launched into a long list of candies that were right for Halloween, and the judge got Spitz to come in and write down the list while I stood there waiting to go to jail.

For the first time in my life, I had no interest in candy.

While Spitz went over the list with my brothers, the judge turned back to me and said he was letting me off. He said I had a good family and nice brothers and should remember that. He figured I wasn't really a criminal and a good family was a better place for me than jail. He wanted to know if I'd tell the neighborhood kids what he'd done, letting me off the hook. I said I would. He said he and Spitz would get better candy for Halloween and hoped we'd come by and not be scared.

And they left.

Coco said I was lucky the judge was a good man. She reminded me what he'd said about our family and my brothers.

I asked if I could have a tuna sandwich and a cup of hot chocolate.

31

Yet Another Note to File

I've been thinking about this for a while. Thought I'd better write it down.

As you know, I grew up in Nashville. My wife, Annie, grew up in Richmond, Virginia. We are both products of Southern culture.

Now, Annie would take issue with that last statement. No self-respecting Richmonder appreciates having her fair city's culture lumped in with Nashville's, as if they were somehow the same. According to Richmonders, Richmond's Southern culture is the real thing—much more refined and genteel than Nashville's. From the perspective of a Richmonder, Nashville's version of Southern culture is tainted with country music, smacks of honky-tonk, and is therefore inferior.

Thankfully, these petty feuds between Southern cities are not relevant to what I'm about to write, so I'm going to lump the various versions of Southern culture together here and just talk about it as a general concept. (I'm begging my Southern friends to forgive me.)

To my way of thinking, Southern culture is mostly defined by two things: Southern food and the Southerner's certain knowledge of "the right way to live."

Now, food is a very positive aspect of Southern culture. We've already spent a good bit of time on it. So, the part of Southern culture I want to talk about here is the right way to live. We Southerners *know* the right way to live. And when you know the right way to live, it is not just okay, it is incumbent upon you to go about doling out great gobs of unsolicited advice to other folks on how they should be living their lives. Knowing the right way to live is a great responsibility.

I cannot speak for Southern girls but I *will* speak for the boys. This is what I know for sure: from the time you are able to understand, most of the grown-ups who take part in your upbringing will impress upon you the great importance of doing well in your studies, excelling at sports, and becoming the president of any organization that will have you, so you can put this important information in your college applications and get into "one of the better schools," preferably a good Southern one.

From your first day at a fine Southern college, you must study the classics and, after four (or sometimes five) years, take a liberal-arts degree on your way to becoming a well-rounded person. At this point you will be prepared for graduate school in medicine, or law, or business. That's it. Three choices: doctor, lawyer, or business tycoon. You may pick any one of the three.

Along the way, you must find a nice girl from a good family and you must court her respectfully. Then you must marry her, and the two of you must have three children.

Producing and bringing forth fewer than three children suggests a bit of marital primness and a cooler-than-truly-Southern current in the blood. Genuine Southern blood is quite warm.

Producing and bringing forth more than three children suggests excess heat in the blood and a certain lack of restraint. Genuine Southerners know how to manage the heat in their blood (my very own parents being notable exceptions to the rule).

Delivering three children into the world demonstrates to onlookers (and there are plenty of them around) an appropriate level of heat in the blood and just the right amount of restraint. It shows good balance in the marital estate.

Once you have your three children, you must go live in a big house in one of the better neighborhoods in town. After you settle into your big house, you must raise your children, encourage them to live the right way, send them off into the world, and wait patiently for your nine grandchildren.

As a reward for living your life the right way, you may then spoil your grandchildren for a while before you die.

This admittedly narrow view of life has its benefits. It produces a well-ordered society of mostly businessmen and lawyers and doctors, almost all of whom marry nice girls from good families who bear promising Southern children, keep up those big houses, and prepare fried chicken, deviled eggs, and Jell-O salads. Such a society has its good points.

To this point, I have lived my life the right way. Except for the grandchildren and dying parts, I've done it all. But there's something missing.

I called Annie. She cut to the chase. "There's nothing wrong with what you've done, Sam. Lord knows, you've got a beautiful, bright, wonderful wife, three great daughters, and a nice life. You ought to be counting your blessings. But there's more to life than living by the rules. That's the part you're missing."

She stopped to think for a minute.

"One time you told me a story about your third-grade teacher. What was her name?"

"Miss Fleming?"

"Right, Miss Fleming. She thought there was more to life than the right way to live, didn't she? Have you thought about her lately?"

"No. Not lately."

"Well, think about her. And by the way, just for the record, that stuff about Richmond and Nashville being the same—culturally, I mean? You know as well as I do that's bunk. They are *not* the same. Not even close. Lordy, Lordy, Lordy, I hope my mother doesn't get her hands on that or you'll be eating Thanksgiving dinner by yourself at a card table in the kitchen."

32

Beautiful Blue Gunk

Live and learn . . .

A long, tall, strikingly beautiful woman, Miss Fleming had raven-black hair and big green eyes framed in red plastic glasses shaped like the wings of a butterfly. Dangling pink hearts, yellow moons, and blue stars tugged at her delicate earlobes. She wore colorful blouses and flowered skirts and sometimes her sparkling red shoes, the ones she called her *Wizard of Oz* shoes.

According to the assessment of parents overheard by us impressionable children, Miss Fleming was a bit of a free spirit. She did not look like a person who was living her life the right way. And while that worried some, it didn't worry them enough to take her away from us kids. Thank goodness.

I had a massive crush on Miss Fleming. All of us boys did. On

Wednesdays, she'd bring her flute to class and play—mostly happy songs but occasionally a tune that'd bring you to the edge of tears on a load of sadness. Miss Fleming could do that to a man; she could train that flute on a fellow's emotions and play them every which way to Sunday.

But, before I go on about Miss Fleming, I need to take a little detour.

In the McLeod household, we had our holiday rituals just like everybody else. You've already read about Christmas Eve, the day before the big day. Well, we also had our own way of doing Christmas Day.

Coco somehow anticipated our first stirrings on Christmas morning, a good bit earlier than was acceptable. She'd show up at our bedroom doors and herd us all into one room, where we were instructed to wait patiently and quietly—something we could not do—while the adults got up, showered, dressed, and assembled around the Christmas tree in the living room with their cups of coffee.

Once the adults had taken up their positions and settled in—a process we judged mostly interminable—Coco reappeared at our holding-room door and announced, "Okay, boys . . ."

She didn't have to finish the sentence. As soon as she cracked the door, we went tearing down a long hall into the living room, where— my, oh my—there were toys as far as the eye could see.

Santa never wrapped our presents like our grandparents did, and there were no names attached to them. Somehow Coco knew what toy went with which boy. She'd stand in the middle of the living room and direct traffic: "Ricky, that's your new tricycle over there . . . Mikey, that's your toy fire engine over there . . ." etc., etc.

Dad camped out behind the movie camera next to the blinding lamp that illuminated the proceedings, recording the event for posterity. We kids scurried around trying out every toy in sight while our grandparents and Wiese looked on and sipped their coffees.

But the Christmas I'm telling you about—the Christmas of my third-grade year—was a little different from those that had gone before, because under the Christmas tree, way in the back, leaning against the wall behind the tree below the picture window, there was one poorly wrapped gift with a scrap of paper taped to the upper left-hand corner of the box. It read "For Sammy."

With some brotherly assistance, I maneuvered the big box into the middle of the living-room floor and looked to Coco for guidance. She seemed perplexed and cut her eyes at Dad, who had a big grin on his face and said, "Go ahead, Sammy. Open your gift."

After the wrapping paper settled onto the floor, I turned the box right side up so we could read the writing on the front. In print big enough for everybody in the room to see, it said YOUNG SCIENTIST'S FIRST CHEMISTRY SET.

Oh, my!

And then everybody in the room turned their attention to the top right-hand corner of the box, where, in smaller print, but still big enough for folks to see, a label read "For ages nine and up."

Uh-oh. I was in the third grade. I was seven years old, almost eight. But I was not nine or up.

Coco's quizzical look turned into an exaggerated frown. Mimi and Wiese followed suit. The ladies in the room were frowning in unison.

I looked back at my dad, who was looking at my mother. His big smile had turned into a smaller, more judicious smile, really just the hint of a smile. Granddaddy McLeod moved in to provide support with a cautious smile of his own.

There were two camps forming, and my elation flipped over into concern.

In situations like this, Coco was the one who most often broke the ice, "Sammy, why don't you boys play with your other toys for a while? Let's leave the chemistry set in the box for the time being. I think the grown-ups need to move on to the kitchen and get breakfast going, where I'D LIKE TO HAVE A WORD WITH YOUR FATHER."

Oh, how I hated those words. Whenever Coco said them, it was not good news for us boys. The chemistry set lay in the middle of the living-room floor looking like a store return. The boy on the box, wearing protective glasses and a scientist's apron, looked like he was waving good-bye.

After a while, Wiese called us in for breakfast. We piled in around the table, the lazy Susan overflowing with country ham biscuits, cheese grits, scrambled eggs, red-eye gravy for those who wanted to sop their biscuits in something, fruit, orange juice, a pitcher of milk, and coffee.

We bowed our heads. Granddaddy said Baptist grace over everything in sight and a whole bunch of things we couldn't see. He slipped in a short reference to casual Christians, begged God not to punish us for being raised Methodist, and suggested that God might want to weigh in on the chemistry-set question, particularly if He felt, as Granddaddy did, that the thing was harmless.

Everybody said, "Amen," except Coco, who said, "Good Lord."

After our plates were loaded and we'd put up with some polite conversation about the quality and dimensions of breakfast, Coco took the floor.

"Sammy," she said, "your father and I have had a discussion about the chemistry set."

A long pause. The breakfast room went quiet, except for Granddaddy, who wanted to know if we had any fig preserves.

"I don't really believe that you're old enough to have a chemistry set," Coco went on, "but your father feels differently."

Another long pause. Nobody moved, except for Granddaddy, who sopped up gravy with a biscuit like nothing was going on.

"So, I have reluctantly agreed that you can keep it."

Harry whooped. Dad smiled and winked. Granddaddy slapped the table hard and rocked back in his chair.

"BUT, there are a few rules."

Before Coco could go on, Granddaddy looked skyward, mouth full of biscuit, and belted out, "Thank you, Jesus."

Then he asked God if He wanted a ham biscuit. "Mighty good, mighty good. Especially with some of this gravy," Granddaddy said. "You sure you don't have any fig preserves?"

Mimi whacked Granddaddy with her napkin and told him to shut his mouth when he chewed.

"Rule one," Coco said. "Sammy, no experimenting in the presence of your brothers. Your brothers are not allowed anywhere near that chemistry set. You hear me? I mean it. First time I catch you conducting an experiment anywhere near one of the other boys, that set is headed to the dump. When you blow yourself to Kingdom Come, you are not taking your brothers with you."

My brothers booed.

"Rule two," she said. "You'll conduct all of your experiments in the shower in our bathroom [meaning my parents' bathroom]. The shower is tiled, floor to ceiling. There's a big drain in the floor. And there's decent lighting. You can keep your chemistry set in the bathroom linen closet. I'll put in a supply of old rags to help with cleanup. Don't be using my nice bath towels for cleanup or I will drown you in the toilet along with your chemicals."

"Rule three," she said. "No school clothes while working with chemicals. Play clothes only."

We waited for more rules, but Coco stopped talking and took a small bite out of her country ham biscuit, signaling end of lecture. Mikey grabbed the last ham biscuit going around the lazy Susan while Ricky complained that he wanted that biscuit and was turning the lazy Susan to get it when Mikey grabbed it. Joey spilled his milk. Wiese got up to get a roll of paper towels. Dad told Mikey to give Ricky half of the biscuit. Mikey said it wasn't fair. Ricky smiled. Granddaddy got ready to say something, but Mimi threatened him with her napkin and he went back to eating with his mouth open.

It all turned out much better than I'd expected.

Every day after school I raced in from the bus stop, changed my clothes, and ran back to the other end of the house and into my parents' bathroom, where I closed and locked the door behind me to keep my brothers out of harm's way. I pulled my chemistry set and a couple of old rags from the linen closet and set up on the floor of the walk-in shower. I fired up my burner and conducted experiments until Coco called us for dinner.

Many of the early experiments ended badly. I had a lot to learn about following a chemistry recipe—selecting the right chemicals, measuring them out properly, combining them at the right times and in the right ways, and heating them just so.

Unfortunately, like I said before, I preferred to learn my lessons the hard way. I made a lot of mistakes. I produced a lot of ugly brown stuff and bad smells.

Occasionally, Coco came all the way from the kitchen, through the breakfast room, down the long hall, through the Big Den, and to the bathroom door, where she'd knock and say, "Sammy, are you okay in there?"

"Yes, ma'am," I'd reply.

"Well, Sammy, what is that bad smell? I can smell it all the way out in the kitchen."

"Yes, ma'am. I bet you can. That last experiment didn't go too well."

"Well, Sammy honey, would you take your pencil and mark in your chemistry book that your mother does not want you ever again to do that experiment in this house? The place smells like a sewer. I will not have my house smelling like a sewer."

And I'd say, "Yes, ma'am." And move on to the next experiment.

That's sort of the way things went for a long time—one mess after another. Until one day . . .

I measured out chemicals just right, poured them into a test tube in just the right way, and heated them just so. The stuff in the test tube started to bubble. Slowly at first. And then more vigorously. And then *poof!* A great white cloud billowed from the top of the tube, gathered up under the ceiling of the shower, and hovered there.

For the first time ever, the smoke didn't smell bad. It actually smelled sort of sweet.

After the smoke cleared, I grabbed the test tube with a pair of tongs and held it up to the light so I could see a glowing blue gel quivering before it settled into a hardened mass—a medium-blue, iridescent residue. Oh, my. It was glorious stuff and it really did glow as if there were a tiny lightbulb burning in the middle of it.

I searched my chemistry set for one of the small cork stoppers that fit in the top of a test tube to keep experiments properly contained. I couldn't find one, so I jumped up off the shower floor and grabbed a big wad of toilet paper, which I twisted and stuffed into the top of the test tube as I ran toward the kitchen to find Coco. She was always in the kitchen.

Now, most of the time when we ran in to show our parents some great new creation, they'd say something like, "Nice job," and then go back to whatever they were doing. Fair enough. It was a reasonable response given that five kids can produce an awful lot of stuff that requires parental approval.

But on this particular day, there in our kitchen, Coco stopped what she was doing and knelt down next to me. She took the test tube in her hands and held it up to the light. And then she said, "Sammy. Oh, my. This is beautiful. What is it?"

And I said I didn't know, but that I'd made it myself and it was the best chemistry experiment so far.

And she agreed.

It was something to behold. It was beautiful blue gunk. I wrapped the test tube in toilet paper and wrapped tape around the toilet paper so that my test tube—half full of beautiful blue gunk—would survive a ride in my book bag.

As luck would have it, the next day was show-and-tell day in Miss Fleming's class. I did not normally have much to show or tell. But on that day I did. I was jumpy with excitement.

When Miss Fleming announced that it was show-and-tell time, a sea of hands filled the air between her and me. I held my left hand as high as I could get it and waved it madly, but Miss Fleming did not look my way. She could be coy like that sometimes.

Sherry sat in the front row right in front of Miss Fleming's desk. Sherry was Miss Fleming's pet and always got called on first. So we all had to listen to whatever Sherry had to say. I don't remember what she talked about but I'm quite sure it wasn't very interesting.

Hands all over the room went up again. I waved my hand in the air. Miss Fleming called on Tom. Tom, who was sweet on Sherry, sat next to her in the front row, and always got called on next. I don't remember what he had to show or tell, probably something he'd made with Lincoln Logs. Whatever it was, I'm sure it was boring.

Hands all over the room went up again. If things kept on this way, I'd never get to show my beautiful blue gunk to the class or Miss Fleming, who'd be so impressed with my inventiveness that she'd decide I was worth waiting for and refuse all suitors until I was grown up and of marriageable age.

But today was another good day for little Sammy McLeod, because Miss Fleming looked right over that sea of hands to find mine and said, "My goodness, Sammy. You don't normally have anything to show or tell. Come on up and share whatever you have there in your book bag."

I bolted to the front of the room, stood next to Miss Fleming's desk, and faced my classmates. I told my story about Christmas, and my chemistry set, and working in the shower where I had my own private chemistry lab, and the bad smells, and what Coco had said.

As I talked, I tore toilet paper from the sides of my test tube. About the time the last shred of toilet paper came away from the test tube and floated to the floor, I got to the part about finally getting an experiment right. I held the test tube up for everybody to see.

My classmates ooh'd and aah'd. They craned their necks to get a better look. Miss Fleming got up from her chair and came up beside me, where she, like Coco, knelt down next to me to get a better look. She smelled like Ivory soap.

She invited the class to come up and gather around us. We peered into the test tube. Folks were mesmerized.

"What is it, Sammy?" Mrs. Fleming asked.

I said, "I don't know but it's pretty and I made it all by myself."

Miss Fleming's eyelids fluttered. Her eyes glistened with tears brimming up, ready to spill over, and her lower lip trembled. I thought I'd said something wrong, but Miss Fleming shook her head until she grabbed control of her emotions and squeaked that she wasn't upset, that it just looked that way, that she was actually as happy as she'd ever been.

"This is a magical day," Miss Fleming said. She pulled a Kleenex from the box on her desk and dabbed at the charcoal-black mascara streaking her cheeks. "Sammy, you have learned something very important about yourself. Just think how much you've loved the chemistry, how hard you've worked at it, how a lot of your experiments failed but how you kept on working at it because you loved it, and never gave up, how you've made this blue gunk, and how beautiful it is. It may turn out to be the most important thing you will ever learn. I hope you'll never forget it. Someday this lesson will be very important to you."

33

Holy Smokes! It's Another Note to File

I just called Annie. Told her I'd been thinking about Miss Fleming and that old story.

"There you go," Annie said. "Now you're getting somewhere. Do what you love. That's a good one. And the bits about family, and friends, and the Hollow, and the food. It all fits.

"Sorry, hon. Gotta run. The horses got loose and are headed west—way west. Better go . . ."

The phone went dead.

34

Weird

The kids in Miss Fleming's classroom were an interesting bunch. But none of them approached Lexi's little brother . . .

Bo Mallory was a weird kid, a kid that only a mother could love, and even she struggled to keep her affection up.

He was small for a four-year-old, towheaded, and devious. Some said mischievous, but Bo's brain dial was set well above mere mischief. He savored opportunities to undermine expectations.

Mrs. Mallory devoted a considerable part of each day to standing on her back porch calling Bo, even though he never responded. After several minutes of hollering, Mrs. Mallory organized the day's search party and dispersed her troops: "Sammy, try the basement. Check inside the washer and the dryer."

Bo had already taken one spin in the dryer. He would have stayed for the full cycle had Mrs. Mallory not noticed the dryer waddling across the cement floor at the end of its electrical cord, Bo making an unbalanced load. You'd have thought he'd be grateful when Mrs. Mallory fished him out. But as soon as he recovered from his dizzy spell, Bo toddled straight back and tried to get the door open.

After that, Mrs. Mallory dried her laundry on the lowest temperature setting. If he got back in somehow, at least he wouldn't get toasted.

"Lexi, check the attic and upstairs. And be sure to hit the crawl space behind the linens on the bottom shelf of the bathroom closet.

"Zeke, you take the first floor and look under all the furniture.

"Chat, you and Possum explore the eastern half of the Hollow down to Sycamore Hill.

"Junior, you and Wiener head west toward the Bradley Smiths'. He may be in Mr. Birdsong's shop. He likes to sniff the glue.

"And everybody meet back here at four o'clock whether you've found him or not."

Mrs. Mallory then hit the phones. Because of kids like Bo and Carrot Top Whitley, the neighborhood had a phone tree before phone trees were fashionable. Mrs. Mallory, wearing her mask of studied calm in the face of likely disaster, alerted moms in the neighborhood to Bo's disappearance. And then she sat on her back steps at command central, dissolved into tears, and commenced her signature hand-wringing. A few more hairs fell from her scalp and her bald spot got a little bigger.

After an hour or so, one of us kids would find Bo. He never said a word or made any move to come out of hiding. He lay curled up wherever you found him, staring at you with his ferret eyes, hissing.

Come to think of it, Bo was a great mimic of animal behavior. Left alone for even a few minutes, the kid somehow scrabbled his way to the top of a high chest or the refrigerator—places the Mallorys' cat,

Hester, frequented. He did the ferret. He did the snake, the fish, and the chicken. (Nobody could figure out where he learned his chicken routine but he had a good one.) He drank from toilets. He ate Charlie, the Mallorys' goldfish, and a handful of aquamarine-blue gravel from the bottom of the fishbowl.

By the time Bo was four, he'd perfected the art of chasing the milk truck. We had a neighborhood egg man, a milkman (Barney), a Krispy Kreme donut man (Roy), a vegetable man, and probably some others I've forgotten. But Bo only chased the milk truck. He was so good at it that Barney threatened to stop deliveries to the Mallorys. Thereafter it was not unusual to see Mrs. Mallory chasing Bo, who was running alongside the Mallorys' dog, Ralph, in hot pursuit of the milk truck, while Mr. Mallory stood on his front porch watching the show, shaking his head, and saying, "That Bo. He's a strange one."

Bo's dog routine developed to the point that he dug holes in the yard and buried his toys instead of leaving them scattered around the house like a normal kid. He crawled on all fours, pawed at doors instead of knocking, and like I said earlier, peed on folks who made him mad.

Bo practiced pyromania. By age six, he had mastered matches and the explosive power of gasoline. He lit his first fire in the Mallorys' tree house. Luckily, Mrs. Mallory managed to get the garden hose on it before it destroyed the tree house and the tree, but rebuilding was a big job. Next he set fire to the Whitleys' yard. Mrs. Whitley and Coco put that fire out with brooms.

And then came Bo's best effort: the Hollow Fire of '59.

Bo dug a bunker in the Mallorys' backyard and set up his army men. He and Ralph the dog lay behind a wall of dirt and waited for an enemy advance. Bo just happened to have a small jelly jar full of gasoline and a few *safety* matches. That's when he developed his own version of a Molotov cocktail. He burned up most of the neighborhood—at least five acres of well-maintained lawn—and attracted the attention of six fire trucks, the fire chief, and two ambulances.

It was another good day in the neighborhood.

Bo Mallory was weird, but entertaining.

35

Running Away

While it was often difficult to understand what prompted Bo to pee on folks, or set fire to things, or run away now and again, there was a time when I understood exactly where he was coming from . . .

The house I grew up in was not all that small, but with five boys stuffed into it, our abode sometimes felt small.

By my ninth birthday, I had outgrown my need for brothers. This was unfortunate because one or more of them followed me everywhere I went. I was the big brother. My younger brothers adored me. Their adoration was, of course, justified; but as a nine-year-old, I needed my space. I did not need an entourage.

This trooping around behind me got so wearisome that I laid down the law. I told Coco that I didn't want the children tagging along with me everywhere I went. Enough was enough. She spent a few minutes explaining how much younger brothers revered older brothers and needed a good role model, and how I was expected to serve as that model and let them come along.

When I said I didn't care, Coco laid down the law and told me it wasn't about me and my brothers would shadow me if they wanted. End of discussion.

We had reached an impasse.

There was only one thing to do: I announced that I was moving out. Running away. But, as a son who'd been raised right, I was letting Coco know my plans just in case she wanted to reconsider.

She didn't.

"You need some help hauling a suitcase out of the attic?" she asked.

I hadn't thought that far ahead. Without the benefit of a plan, I said, "I'll just grab the old blanket off the foot of my bunk and load my stuff into the middle of it and sling it over my back like the hobos do."

"How long will you be gone?" she asked.

"Forever," I said. "But I plan to visit from time to time. I'm not going away mad. I'm just going out on my own a little earlier than I'd planned."

"Fine," Coco said. "How about some peanut-butter-and-jelly sandwiches for the road? Better take at least two, don't you think? You want me to do a little laundry real quick to make sure you have enough clean underwear?"

I said I'd pass on the clean underwear but a couple of sandwiches might come in handy.

"And," she said, "one last question: Do you have any idea where you'll be staying?"

"No, ma'am," I said. "I don't. I'll have to figure that out once I hit the road."

Then she said, "Write, if you get the chance."

"Yes, ma'am, I will. I'll throw in a pencil and a piece of paper."

My brothers watched me roll my pillow, my cowboy hat, my rock collection, a T-shirt, and an extra pair of jeans into the blanket. When I told them I was moving out, I thought they'd beg me to stay. They didn't.

By four o'clock, I was packed and headed for the door. Coco came running from the kitchen yelling for me to wait just a minute. I had to chuckle to myself. Now she was going to do what she should have done from the beginning—beg me to stay and promise that my brothers would never, ever, follow me again unless I wanted them to.

She didn't.

She took my face in her hands, gave me a kiss on the forehead, said she hoped I'd find the freedom I craved, and then opened the door so I could be on my way.

My brothers crowded into the doorway around her and watched me walk down the driveway. As Coco closed the door, I could hear Joey shouting at Ricky that he claimed my bunk.

When I crossed the Big Road, I looked back to see if anyone was watching me from the house. Nope, nobody was watching.

It was a late October day. The sky was clouding up and spitting a few fat drops of rain now and again. Tight gusts of wind pushed fallen leaves down Moccasin Creek and rippled its surface. A squall was coming, so I hotfooted it down to Sycamore Hill and settled in underneath the bridge before things got bad.

I laid my baby-blue blanket out on the rocks under the bridge and managed to get a corner of it mashed down in a big pile of fresh dog doo. Scraping it off the blanket with a flat rock took a while.

By the time I was done, rain pounded the creek bed around me. Possum's dog, Diesel, who roamed like he didn't belong to anybody, came running toward me, shook a bucketful of dog smell onto me and my blanket, and nosed his way to my sandwiches. I snatched 'em off the blanket before Diesel got 'em.

I told Diesel what was happening. I was running away and the two peanut-butter sandwiches were all the food I had in the world. I hadn't even thought to bring a canteen of Kool-Aid and would probably end up drinking out of the creek like he did. I was glad to have his company and would give him a corner of a sandwich, but that was it. There were limits to my hospitality.

There we sat. Diesel lay on the blanket with his head in my crotch, looking up at me with his black eyes, licking his chops every time I took a bite of my sandwich, hoping that I'd give up more than I'd promised. Which I did.

We ate the first sandwich in nothing flat and decided, Diesel and me, that we might as well go on and eat the other one, too.

It rained pretty steady for the next hour or so. It got dark. The wind blew cold rain up under the bridge. The dog doo smelled to high heaven. Even Diesel thought so. But neither of us was leaving until the rain let up.

Diesel heard it before I did. His head came up out of my lap and his ears flipped forward to let more sound in. I strained to hear whatever it was that had him on point. Hair stood up on the back of my neck and my arms broke out in goose pimples. But I couldn't see anything and couldn't hear anything except the rain and the wind in the weeds at the edge of the bridge. It was dark-dark. Not even moonlight.

And then I heard it. Something growled and thrashed around at the edge of the creek. Diesel tore out from under the bridge at the noise and I tore out from under the bridge the other way as fast as I could. Maybe faster.

I sprinted down the Big Road, across the Whitleys' yard, and up our driveway to the back porch. I stood there fighting for air, waiting for the shaking to stop. I was sopping wet. But I didn't go in. I had to get my story straight in my head. It wouldn't do to say I was scared witless and had run home.

When I went in the Little Den door, my brothers were running miniature cars off the coffee table, tilting it up at one end by putting shoes under the table legs, rolling the cars down the slope into a wooden bowl. It looked like fun.

Coco was sitting on the tweed-brown sofa—the one that didn't show dirt—darning a pair of Mikey's jeans and keeping score for the car game.

I tried to look cool, like nothing out of the ordinary was going on. I said I'd forgotten my rain jacket, had run out of peanut-butter sandwiches, and needed to find my canteen and fill it with Kool-Aid.

Ricky claimed the canteen was his, but Coco took my side. She said my stuff hadn't been officially distributed among the remaining brothers. I could still claim it if I needed it. Which I did.

"You want any help with the sandwiches or the Kool-Aid?" Coco asked.

"No, ma'am," I said, and went off to find my jacket and collect provisions.

Back in the Little Den, I announced that I'd decided to hang out for a while and play with those cars and maybe even stay for supper before heading out again.

Nobody seemed to care one way or the other, although Ricky was still whining about the canteen.

Coco just smiled and went to fix supper. "You sure you want to eat with us? I can make you a few more peanut-butter sandwiches if you need to get on with your independence."

I said I figured my independence could wait until after supper.

Joey said he figured I was just a chicken and scared of the dark, so I popped him one.

Over supper, Coco told Dad all about my independence and moving out. He wanted to know where I was headed and where I was staying and what I was eating and so on and so forth. I told him about the dog doo and the rain and the growling noise.

I wasn't too hungry for supper, having just eaten most of two peanut-butter sandwiches, but it was sort of nice to be back in the house, sitting at our big table, the lazy Susan piled high with ham and peas and mashed potatoes and gravy and biscuits.

By the time Coco dished up the vanilla ice cream and ladled on some hot fudge sauce, I had lost the itch for independence, so I told her I might just stay for a few more days.

"That'd be nice," she said.

36

Goblins Gone Wild

Running away was scary, but not as scary as Halloween . . .

It was the year Halloween came on a Saturday—a whole day and night of Halloween.

Our McLeod relatives came from Jackson to join in the festivities and see us in our Halloween outfits and Dad came home early from his Saturday hospital rounds. Coco was overjoyed.

"I could use a few extra hands this weekend," she said.

Early that Saturday morning, Granddaddy McLeod and I went shopping for my Halloween costume. My brothers already had theirs. They'd figured out what they wanted to be weeks before the big day and Coco had bought what she needed to outfit them, but I'd been slow to make a decision and Coco had thrown up her hands, saying I'd have to come up with something on my own. So, when

Granddaddy McLeod heard I didn't have a costume, he said he'd take me to get one and Coco said, "Hallelujah," or something like that.

Coco had bought Joey a pumpkin outfit—really just a large orange plastic ball with a few black lines running down its sides and the necessary holes for human appendages. It looked more like a basketball than a pumpkin.

According to Coco, she'd saved a lot of money on Joey's costume because he could wear the big plastic thing over his green pajamas—the ones with the feet in them. She figured the pumpkin would cover the spaghetti stains. She'd make him a headband out of old panty hose, orange construction paper, and leaves from the yard, so his head would look like the top of a pumpkin.

Joey pitched a fit. He said he wanted the pumpkin costume he'd picked out, not the awful-looking thing Coco'd bought and he wasn't wearing panty hose on his head. If he had to wear the orange ball, he was skipping Halloween. But Coco said he was going to wear it because she'd spent a lot of time on it and he'd look cute in it and she wanted pictures of us in our costumes to send to our Jolley relatives.

At that, Joey pulled a page from Coco's playbook and took to his bed.

Ricky was going to be Superman . . . again. He was Superman every year. You'd have thought that meant he could wear the same outfit the next year if he hadn't outgrown it, but he flew around the yard in his costume every day for months after Halloween and always wore the thing out.

One winter, he got so thoroughly caught up in his character that he jumped off the top of the swing set, thinking he could fly. He couldn't. He got a broken leg and a chocolate bar from Dr. Pritchard to show for it.

Harry was going to be the Road Runner. He wore his brown pajamas with the feet in them, brown-construction-paper wings

Wiese pinned on for him, and the fingers of a Playtex Living Glove stretched over his head—what Wiese called his "rooster comb." He spent the entire day running around the house yelling "BEEP BEEP."

Mikey was going as a baby, which he was. Coco found an old rattle for him. He was happy banging it on everything in sight and seemed to think he was participating, even though the rest of us knew he wasn't.

When Granddaddy and I came home with a new Indian outfit, everybody but Joey gathered around to see it. It was something—a real bow, real wooden arrows with metal tips (not suction cups), leggings and a vest made out of real leather, brand-new leather moccasins, and a headdress of genuine simulated eagle feathers that flowed down my back. Granddaddy whispered to Mimi that he'd spent a pretty penny on it.

Hearing all the hoopla, Joey got out of bed long enough to take one look at my elaborate costume, take another look at his pumpkin outfit, feel himself thoroughly slighted, and go back to bed.

Coco didn't seem all that happy with my outfit, either. She stood looking at Granddaddy and me like we'd done something wrong, but she didn't say anything.

That afternoon, while I was practicing with my bow and arrows in the backyard, Zeke suddenly appeared.

"Can I shoot one?" he asked as we watched one of my arrows disappear into the gray-black clouds above our heads, just this side of outer space.

Zeke and I counted when we lost sight of the arrow "one . . . two . . ." and strained to see it as it reappeared. It looked like a tiny black dot at first, then gradually grew larger, and plummeted back toward the ground, stabbing the earth just a few feet from where we stood, burying its metal tip in dense Tennessee red clay.

Zeke grabbed the arrow and tugged a couple of times before it came free. We studied the hole it left in the dirt—a couple of inches deep.

"Jammers," Zeke said.

(Zeke was always trying to invent stuff, like the next catchy neighborhood word. Instead of "cool," he said "jammers" until everybody told him "jammers" wasn't cool.)

"How fast do you think that thing was going when it hit the ground?" I asked.

As you may remember, Zeke was an Erector-set kind of guy. He knew these things, mostly because he watched a lot of Mr. Wizard shows on TV. And when he didn't know the answer to a technical question, he wasn't above making something up.

"Often wrong, but never in doubt," Mr. Mallory said. "That kid's going somewhere in this life."

Zeke stood for a minute, rubbing his chin, looking up at the sky before answering. He licked his finger with his tongue and held it up to get a sense of the wind speed. He wondered aloud about barometric pressure.

"What?" I asked.

"Barometric pressure," he repeated. "The speed of the arrow is a function of the distance it traveled into the clouds, gravity, wind direction, and air density."

"I just want to know how fast it was going," I said again.

"About a hundred miles an hour," Zeke said in an authoritative voice. He looked at me from behind his thick black-framed glasses—the ones held together with a paper clip where a screw had come out—to see if I was buying it.

I was.

"Holy moly!" I said. "A hundred miles an hour."

"Yep, at least a hundred miles an hour. Maybe faster."

Just how far could he go with this?

"Could be a thousand miles an hour," Zeke opined. "Hard to say."

We let the wonder of it sink in for a bit before Zeke looked back at me and asked again, in a very polite way, if he could shoot the next arrow.

That was a tough question.

Zeke didn't often stoop to play with me, or any other neighborhood kids for that matter. I was a whole year younger and he was, according to himself, a whole lot smarter and too busy inventing stuff. This was the first time he'd taken a real interest in me. He said he wouldn't have come over to my house if he hadn't seen me shooting arrows into the ether. I didn't want to disappoint him.

But I had a quiver full of real wooden arrows with real feathers on them, and a real wooden bow slung over my shoulder. My headdress full of genuine simulated eagle feathers was insanely good-looking. I knew I looked cool because I'd spent a lot of time admiring myself in Coco's full-length mirror. I was not the kind of kid who looked cool very often, so I was reluctant to give up my new accessories.

Plus, Dad said my new bow and the metal-tipped arrows could be dangerous. He said I was old enough to be smart about it, but I needed to be careful. He said somebody could get hurt and I shouldn't be shooting the thing when other people were around.

That was the opening Coco was looking for. She said if anybody got hurt, she'd take my bow and shoot an arrow right through my head and we'd see how I liked it.

Looking back now, there were a lot of good reasons not to let Zeke fire the next arrow into outer space, but I handed him the bow and a brand-new arrow anyway. Like I said, I did a lot of stupid things as a kid.

The arrow took off like it had been fired from a cannon. It was going so fast it whistled as it disappeared into the clouds. Once again we strained to see it. This time we counted "one . . . two . . . three . . . four" before we saw it again, just that tiny little speck. Zeke was setting some sort of new record.

The thing came barreling back toward the earth. We held our

breath and watched it change from a tiny black dot into a real wooden arrow and then, just before the thing buried itself in the ground . . . THUNK!

It stuck right in the top of Chat's head. He'd shown up from no-where.

"Ouch," hollered Chat.

"Jammers," said Zeke.

Chat reached up and pulled the arrow from his head. Blood spurted like water from a geyser.

I guess you could say things worked out better than I had any right to hope.

According to Dr. Pritchard, the arrow lodged itself firmly in Chat's cranium—a bone God put in Chat's head to keep arrows and things of that sort from sticking in his brain.

Chat lost a lot of blood and had to stay in the hospital overnight "for observation," but there was no lasting damage.

Dr. Pritchard said he'd be fine.

That was a relief because Mrs. Witherspoon said if the arrow had gotten to Chat's brain, he'd probably have had to get an operation and stay in the hospital for a long time, and then, after he got better, he'd probably have had to ride the short bus to a special school. Chat said he didn't want to go to a special school.

Zeke was confined to his room for a week and never played with me again.

Coco didn't shoot an arrow through my head to find out how I liked it. She threatened to, but she didn't. Instead, I was confined to my room for a week, same as Zeke.

Granddaddy McLeod hid in the recliner in the den with his nose stuck in the newspaper while Coco, Mimi, and Wiese gave him the cold shoulder.

The bow and arrows went into the trash, but not until after Coco stood in front of Granddaddy McLeod in his recliner, with Wiese and Mimi standing behind her, and broke everything in half.

That's when Dad said he was taking Joey, Ricky, Harry, and baby Mikey trick-or-treating. It was not the kind of thing my dad normally did, but it was a good decision. Hanging around the house with Granddaddy did not seem like a very smart thing to do.

Joey wore my new Indian outfit that night, but without the confiscated bow-and-arrow accessories. I watched him walk out the door. He looked good, but not totally cool.

When he got home afterward, he said a lot of people had liked *his* costume. He figured he'd gotten extra candy because of it, but he never shared any with me. For the rest of that evening, he and Ricky took turns opening the door to my room, dangling their bags full of candy in front of me, pulling them back, slamming the door, and laughing like hyenas.

In case you're wondering, Judge Berkeley and Spitz handed out Three Musketeers candy bars—big ones—that Halloween night. Joey, Ricky, Harry, and Mikey each got one. So did Dad. According to Ricky, the judge had asked where I was.

"He's stuck in his room. Coco won't let him out 'cause he shot a guy in the head with an arrow," Ricky said.

"That's too bad," the judge said.

"No it's not," Joey said, smoothing the genuine simulated eagle feathers on his headdress.

37

On the Road

Jackson, Tennessee

I arrived in Jackson at dusk and stopped for gas.

While I was wiping bug goo from the windshield, Jolie, our middle daughter, called—all the way from New York City.

Jolie gets her coffee at the same corner deli every morning, teaches kindergarten from dawn till dusk at an inner-city school, has a personal trainer named Maximillian, plays coed sports with twentysomethings year-round, goes out every night, and loves her hectic life.

"Well, it's about time," I said.

"What?"

"If you're calling about my girlfriend, you're a little late. Your mom and sisters are way ahead of you."

"So you're admitting it now?"

"I'm not admitting anything," I said.

"You just called her your girlfriend."

"We never dated," I said.

"Yeah, that's what Summer said you'd say. So when's the picnic?"

"Day after tomorrow."

"You still worrying about your looks?"

"No, I'm not worrying about my looks anymore. Not much, anyway."

"Well, I wouldn't if I were you," Jolie said. "You're better-looking than most old guys. Hey, gotta run, Dad. Tell Wiese and Coco I said hello . . . and what's-her-name, too."

"Lexi," I said.

I pulled up in front of Wiese's old folks' home near the hospital. I figured we'd find a comfortable spot in the visiting room and have a nice chat. Maybe we'd get a little something to eat in the cafeteria if she had her appetite.

But there she was, ninety-one years young, sitting in a rocker on the front porch, party purse in hand, coiffed, eyelashes attached, cheeks rouged, red dress on, her walker folded up and leaning on the porch rail.

I wasn't surprised. "Goin' out" has always been at the top of Wiese's list.

She gave me a big hug. I could feel her struggling to hold on to me, thin frail bones shaking with effort. She patted me on the top of my head just like she'd always done, after I bent down so she could reach it.

"My gracious me, Sam! You are one sight for sore eyes and still growing. Out, not up. Ha ha. That was a good one, wasn't it? Haven't lost your sense of humor, have you?"

"Wiese, you sure you're up for goin' out? We don't have to go out. We can grab something to eat here if you like."

"Lawd, honey, I wouldn't miss this for the world. I'm not stuck in a grave yet. Take those durned tennis balls off my walker, will you? Thing won't half roll with the durned tennis balls on it.

"Do I look like . . . what's that boy's name? McEnroe? I don't know what the durned people 'round here are thinkin'. Tennis balls on old folks' walkers.

"What d'you want to eat?" she inquired. And then before I could say anything: "I want a steak. You still like steak?" She moved her high heels and walker toward the car.

"Well, sure," I said. "I like steak. But what about your doctor? What does he say? A steak will be full of fat and high on salt. Salt's not on your program."

"Program. Is that what you call it? Bunk. What my doctor doesn't know won't hurt him. He isn't coming to dinner. I'm havin' a steak. And a glass of wine. I've been lookin' forward to a glass of red wine. My, my, won't that be fine. And don't you be squeelin' to the durned doctor about me drinkin' one measly glass of wine."

We had steak and a glass of wine. Talked family, old times, and food—chicken deluxe, coconut cake, boiled custard, strawberry pie.

Same ol' Wiese.

After dinner, we went back to her room—a quiet, peaceful place. We fished through her recipe box, and found some family favorites. "I'm giving you these durned recipes," she said. "Got no use for 'em anymore. Best you hold on to 'em. Not much time . . ."

Her voice trailed off. She fingered the food-splattered cards, then handed them to me, pressed them into my hands with both of hers, and looked at me, eyes unblinking.

"Some get statues and some get roads named after 'em," she said. "But I'm going on to my reward knowing you boys are still eating my strawberry pie and that's way better than getting a road with my name on it."

Wiese's Strawberry Pie

Serves 8

Ingredients

8 cups strawberries

$^2/_3$ cup sugar

$^2/_3$ cup water

2 tablespoons cornstarch

1 baked pie shell (homemade, if you're up to it)

CUT the tops from the strawberries and cut in half.

IN a blender, blend one cup strawberries and the water until smooth.

IN a pot, combine sugar, cornstarch, and contents of blender. Cook over medium heat and bring to a slow boil for a few minutes, stirring frequently until the mixture is nicely thickened.

LET the glaze cool. Then coat the pie shell with enough of the glaze to cover the bottom and sides.

TOSS the remaining strawberries and glaze in a large bowl until the strawberries are well coated. Then pour the berries into the pie shell and chill for a couple of hours in the refrigerator before serving.

THIS is special!

38

Hoodlums

You may remember that I called the Hollow a "peaceful place." Most of the time that was true, but occasionally . . .

It was May. I'm pretty sure of that. I say May because that's when we got the best winds in our little valley, the very best time of year for kite flying.

The days were getting longer and we neighborhood kids looked forward to the end of the school year. We each bought a Hi-Flier paper kite and a couple of balls of string—ten cents for the diamond-shaped paper kite and about ten cents for each ball of string, maybe thirty cents for the whole shooting match. Mr. Birdsong helped us assemble our kites. He dabbed extra wood glue where the cross-sticks met. We were ready to fly.

All of the kids flew their kites in our front yard, where there were no trees of any consequence and no telephone lines to snatch a kite out of the sky and rip it to shreds. Dodging other kids' kites was hard enough.

The more aggressive among us tested the wills and wallets of the timid by dancing our kites up close to see whether they'd flinch or not. A kid who'd emptied a piggy bank to buy his kite was going to be reluctant to tangle with you. Some were simply more frugal and unwilling to lose a kite in a test of wills, even if piggy banks were full. So the poverty-stricken and timid among us tended to fly on the fringes while the reckless battled it out in the middle with kites on either side of them.

Only rarely did a kite last more than a day or two if flown in the thick of things; flown on the fringes, it might survive a week if all went well. The only certainty was that sooner or later you'd be asking your mom for extra chores to earn the next thirty cents for a trip to Beasley Hardware.

One cloudy, blustery afternoon, Possum showed up with a brand-new plastic box kite. It was a brightly colored job on a sturdy wood frame. Mr. Birdsong had reinforced the corners with short wooden dowels and plenty of glue. It was the kind of kite that required a stiff wind for flight.

I had only seen one before. Mr. Mallory and Zeke flew theirs too near the sun and the heat burned through the kite string. That kite blew all the way to China. At least that's what Mr. Mallory claimed.

So when Joey and I spied Possum in our front yard with that fancy kite, we sprinted headlong into wind gusts strong enough to knock less solid boys off their feet.

Possum said his uncle had given him the kite and he'd stored it on the top shelf of his closet, just waiting for the right day. Possum also gave us some cock-and-bull story about how his uncle said only Possum should fly it on account of the fact that he was special and understood the finer points of kite flying and wouldn't make a mess of things.

After Possum tied on the extra-strong kite string recommended by Mr. Beasley, he handed Joey the kite, told him he'd pound him if he broke it, and backed into the wind, letting out string so the kite could take off. When Possum gave the signal, Joey hurled that kite into the wind and the thing sailed skyward, taking string as fast as Possum fed it.

The kite climbed so high that, within minutes, it was just a dark speck in an otherwise gray sky. It was so high that we could see the lower edges of the clouds pass between us and the kite. Honest.

Now, as you can imagine, Joey and I begged Possum to let us fly that kite. We may not have been convincing, but what we lacked in persuasiveness we made up for with persistence. Yet no matter how forcefully we pleaded, Possum wasn't giving up the string. So, there we stood, watching Possum fly the kite of our dreams, unable to do anything but say "wow" every few seconds as the kite danced in and out of the clouds.

Joey lost interest before I did and headed for the house. The sky spat rain and the wind picked up. As I turned and headed for the house, Possum grabbed his wiener, moaned that he had to pee, handed me the kite string, and ran across the Big Road into the woods hollering over his shoulder that he'd boink me if I lost his kite while he was gone. He'd be right back, he said.

The wind was blowing leaves and twigs in great swirls around the yard. The kite tugged on its string harder than I'd ever felt before. It danced left if you pulled the string to the left. It'd circle to the right if you looped the string to the right in a big arc. It was kite-flying joy like I'd never experienced, and it made me long for a box kite of my very own. While I waited on Possum to pee, I tried to do the math in my head, to figure out what the kite and all that string would cost.

Pretty soon, here came Possum, walking back across the Big

Road headed my way. He had a handful of gravel and was mindlessly tossing rocks, one by one, into the middle of the road, acting very Possum-like.

As he crossed the road, a white Volkswagen Beetle with a black convertible top came roaring around the Big Curve, playfully swerving in Possum's direction, intending to scare him into jumping out of the way. Possum didn't budge. Instead he backhanded a few pebbles at the Beetle. I could hear the rocks pinging off the side of the car.

The Beetle came to a skidding stop and two extra-large teenagers piled out. One wore a Nashville Dells baseball cap and a black leather Elvis jacket. The other had a crew cut and looked like a professional wrestler. They ran full tilt after Possum, who ran toward me, then past me, and around the corner of our house and out of sight, leaving me, ten-year-old Sammy McLeod, to suffer the wrath of extra-large teenagers hopped up on testosterone.

The wrestler tore the kite string from my hand and made a big show of throwing it to the wind, howling like a madman.

Possum's box kite took off for points east. Way east. Like France, maybe.

Possum hollered from the corner of our house that he was going to boink me, and disappeared again.

The bully in the baseball cap grabbed the tail of my jacket and swung me in whirligig circles. If I didn't tell them the name of the kid who'd pummeled their car with gravel, they were going to beat me to a bloody pulp and leave me to die.

It was a difficult situation. I thought briefly—very briefly—about protecting Possum. I told the bully that I was just a ten-year-old kid and not worth the effort he was putting into me. And when that didn't slow him down, information poured out of me like water from a fire hose. Between moans, I told everything I knew about Possum Bradley Smith, including where he lived, what time he arrived at the bus stop, and where they could find him after school. I ratted on

Possum so fast I could hardly catch my breath. I was still flying around in circles and starting to feel a little nauseous.

And then, as if on cue, here came the moms.

I might have died that day. I might never have seen Rock City, or eaten gravlax on toast points garnished with a few sprigs of dill, or had sex. My life could easily have ended seriously unfulfilled. But the moms saved me.

Mrs. Littlejohn stormed across her yard in bright red high heels and a silky white sleeveless dress. Coco flew off the front steps of our house, apron on, slicing the air with a wooden soup spoon. Mrs. Whitley, hair in curlers netted in place, ran down our driveway brandishing a can of Lysol.

The baseball-capped teenager who was spinning me like a top dropped me like a hot potato and sprinted back to the Beetle after his buddy, and the two of them jumped in and took off.

Coco stood over me with her soup spoon asking if I was okay while Mrs. Whitley recited the license-plate number of the Beetle over and over to herself so she wouldn't forget it. Possum ran from the bushes screaming that I'd let go of his kite and was going to get boinked. Mrs. Whitley, a little frustrated by all of this, squirted Possum in the face with Lysol and told him to shut the $@&* up. (Nice language, Mrs. Whitley!)

Coco pulled me off the ground while Mrs. Littlejohn brushed the grass out of my hair. Possum used his shirttail to wipe Lysol out of his eyes and went running home—the long way, through neighborhood backyards, to avoid the Beetle. After her little rage, Mrs. Whitley, somewhat predictably, forgot the Beetle's license number, said "$@&*" again right out loud, and walked off muttering about hoodlums.

The next day up at the Cave, Possum told Lexi and Chat how I'd ratted him out. He said he was probably going to get killed by those hoodlums the next time they saw him. He sat dejectedly on Pee

Rock, shook his head, and speculated aloud about where his box kite had ended up . . . how it might have fallen into some other neighborhood . . . how it didn't have his name on it . . . finders keepers . . . and how lucky some kid was . . . some kid who'd probably found that kite blowing around in his yard . . . that is, if it hadn't gotten caught in a tree . . . or chewed up by some dog.

39

Bombing the Beetle

And that wasn't the end of it . . .

After the "incident," the neighborhood bristled with heightened security.

Coco took it upon herself to inform the uninformed that our little piece of the universe had been infiltrated by undesirables: teenage boys, speeding around in a white Volkswagen Beetle with a black convertible top, looking for trouble.

Mrs. Whitley's all-too-regular memory lapse meant there'd be no tracking the Beetle by its license plate, but the moms present at the "incident" were pretty sure there was a Hillwood High School decal in the rear window, or at least that's the way Mrs. Littlejohn remembered it.

Next day, Mrs. Littlejohn drove around the high school parking lot looking for the offending vehicle. She didn't find it.

Mrs. Mallory called the assistant principal and asked whether the school had any record of the car. They didn't.

Mrs. Bradley Smith dealt with the "incident" by grounding Possum *and* Junior, even though Junior had been nowhere near the "incident." She said Possum deserved grounding and Junior should not be wandering the neighborhood if there were hoodlums at large.

Mrs. Turner Smith ordered Wiener to walk through backyards on his way to our house and stay off the roads. She also reported the "incident" to Judge Berkeley, thinking he might order extra patrols of the neighborhood and initiate an investigation. He didn't, but he said he'd alert Spitz to look out for the Beetle.

And, of course, Mrs. Whitley stocked up on Lysol and told Bobby to stay in his room with the blinds pulled. She would have told the same to Carrot Top but knew very well that she'd be wasting one of the precious breaths God had allotted her.

Mrs. Whitley figured it was only a matter of time until Carrot Top found the Beetle, called the hoodlums unmentionable names, got the tar beat out of him, and ended up in the gutter with life-threatening lacerations. If history was any guide, somebody would find him just in time to get him to Dr. Pritchard, who would sew him up and fill him with blood donated by Church Street drunks dying from venereal disease.

Mrs. Whitley had a vivid imagination for disaster, and anybody who knew Carrot Top understood why. Most of the things Mrs. Whitley worried about came true.

Inside of a week, the Beetle was the stuff of legend among us neighborhood kids. Visions of the Bug loomed larger in our frontal lobes than anything we saw on *Shock Theater*, larger than Frankenstein or Dracula. We talked about the Beetle like it was some jagged-toothed monster prowling for kid meat.

Possum saw the Beetle in his dreams. He described hoodlums stalking him, leering through the front windshield, shaking their fists at him from open windows, honking the Beetle's squeaky horn at him. One night the Beetle appeared at Possum's bedroom door but couldn't squeeze through. Junior screamed from the Beetle's backseat that the hoodlums had him and were going to beat him senseless if Possum didn't hand himself over. That's when Possum woke up sweating, or at least, that's what Possum said. Junior said Possum wet the bed and screamed for his momma like a baby.

I was something of an authority on the Beetle, having seen it and the hoodlums up close. I told anybody who'd listen about the rattle-snake tattoos on the hoodlums' forearms, the cigarette packs rolled up in their T-shirt sleeves, and the motorcycle logos on their hoodlum jackets. Chat wondered how I could have seen the tattoos and ciga-rette packs if the hoodlums were wearing jackets. Admittedly, it was hard to keep the various versions of the story straight.

A few days later, Lexi flew into the Cave, waving her arms, whisper-yelling that the Beetle was coming down Sycamore Hill. We all saw it, the white Beetle with the black convertible top, careening down Sycamore Hill Road. Two blonde-haired girls, no hoodlums.

News of the Beetle sighting spread like wildfire through our neigh-borhood. I slept over at Chat's house that night. We overheard Mrs. Witherspoon talking to Mrs. Whitley on the phone. She said the Beetle full of hoodlums had its top down, so you could get a good look at them, at least six teenage boys. It sped right through the in-tersection below the bridge without even slowing down. Thank good-ness no other car was coming down the Big Road, because somebody would surely have been killed.

Chat and I knew only one little part of that story was true, but we liked her story better than the truth and she had a way of telling it that made your skin crawl.

From that day forward, the Crockett Rangers of Nashville, Ten-nessee, were on the case. One of us kids stood lookout by the Cave entrance every afternoon.

Possum and Junior sometimes had a babysitter named Lucille.

They didn't mind having a sitter if it was Lucille, because she was sixteen or seventeen and had boobs. Possum said if you sat next to Lucille on the sofa and looked through the buttons on her shirt, you could see where her boobs disappeared into her bra, but not the nipples.

"I saw a nipple once," Junior said.

"Nuh-uh," Possum said.

"Uh-huh," Junior yelled. "I saw one once when you weren't looking."

"Nuh-uh," Possum said.

"Oh, brother," Lexi said.

Anyway, Lucille was reading a book to Possum and Junior about some boys in a club like the Crockett Rangers (except there were no girls).

"They set traps in the woods to catch invaders," Possum said.

We Crockett Rangers were at our best when we had a good project to work on. The late-spring days were warm and sunny, perfect for booby-trapping an entire hillside.

Mr. Witherspoon gave us some rope. Mr. Mallory pitched in with some rope and cardboard. He also let us borrow his safety knife. Lexi said she'd carry the knife so her dad could rest easy that nobody would get hurt. (Lexi was sounding more like a mom every day.) My dad said he'd doctor us if one of us got hurt, but he was fresh out of rope.

We booby-trapped like our lives depended on it. Along the south bank of Moccasin Creek, we pulled the tops of small saplings down to the water. We tied short ropes into the tops of the trees and the other ends of the ropes around loose flat rocks. When an interloper disturbed a booby-trapped rock, a sapling would spring like a whip and whack him.

Uphill, between the creek and the Cave, we dug a series of holes three feet deep and two feet square and covered them with flats of cardboard. We camouflaged the cardboard with leaves. Near the holes, we set more sapling traps.

We even set a sapling trap in the middle of No-Man's-Land, below Pee Rock. Junior and I washed our hands and tennis shoes in the creek after we installed that one.

We invited Carrot Top to the Cave one afternoon so we could see how well those traps worked. He fell into a hole and twisted his ankle so badly that Chat and I had to help him home. Until that day, Carrot Top had refused to join our club because we teased him about pooing in the Cave. But after he experienced our handiwork, he changed his tune and begged us to let him in.

And that is how the Crockett Rangers of Nashville, Tennessee, grew from five to six members. We let him in even though the Wheaties promotion was over and Carrot Top couldn't get a bag of dirt or a certificate.

It was late June before we saw the Beetle again. It topped the hill and lurched toward Sycamore Hill Bridge with its black convertible top down. There were two blonde girls in the front seat, both with long ponytails. And there were two teenage boys in the backseat, one of them sitting up on the edge of the folded convertible top with his arms extended like he was flying. The radio in the Beetle blared and the boys sang at the tops of their lungs.

The next day about the same time, the Beetle came flying down the hill again, this time with the boys in the front and the girls in the back.

And the next day. And the next day. And so on and so forth, until it dawned on us kids that we were observing a pattern.

While we watched for the Beetle and maintained our booby traps, we noticed that the Osage orange trees were developing their fruit earlier than usual. Carrot Top, who took fortifications seriously, said we should collect a bunch of the grapefruit-size green mushy fruits, so we could bomb the hoodlums if they got past the booby traps and came to ransack the Cave.

Lexi puffed herself up and said, "We don't need those smelly oranges in our cave. You can't join our club and start giving orders."

Carrot Top said Lexi was just a stupid girl and he didn't want to be a member of a wimpy club that didn't have any bombs. He said pretty soon, once we got our act together under his leadership, we'd have plenty to ransack and would need the nasty Osage oranges to attack our enemies and protect the Cave.

Chat said, "Who elected you?"

And Carrot Top said, "Nobody yet, but you will. When we get this place fortified, you'll see what I'm talking about and you'll want to make me president or something."

Lexi said, "Oh, brother."

It didn't take long for us to build a pile of overripe oranges in the Cave. When the Cave was properly fortified, Carrot Top stalked around like he owned the place, barking orders at Possum and Junior to head uphill, hide by the road, whistle if they saw the Beetle coming. He put Lexi in charge of the Cave, saying girls should not be out on the front lines.

Lexi looked like she was going to spit.

Carrot Top grabbed three or four Osage oranges and started off down the hill. He ordered Chat and me to follow him.

"Who elected you?" Chat said again.

Carrot Top ignored him and ran down the hill.

Chat stalked off, saying he was sick of being in a club with a bully.

Carrot Top yelled, "Good riddance."

I followed Carrot Top even though Chat was my best friend. In retrospect, not one of my better decisions.

When we arrived at Sycamore Hill Bridge, we crossed the creek. Carrot Top tucked two slimy Osage oranges under his T-shirt and stuffed the tail into his pants. Green stuff soaked through his shirt but that didn't bother Carrot Top. A little slime was nothing to him.

He climbed into a big old oak tree next to the bridge and scooted out on a fat branch above the road.

"What are we doing?" I yelled.

"Laying for the Beetle," he said.

Since I didn't know what "laying for the Beetle" meant and didn't have anything else to do, I hunkered down in the weeds at the base of the tree and waited.

We hadn't been there but maybe five minutes before Possum and Junior commenced a duet of ear-piercing whistles. Sure enough, here came the Beetle, careening downhill, convertible top down, radio blaring, hoodlums in the front seat, blonde girls in back, ponytails blowing every which way in the wind.

As the Beetle screeched to a stop at the stop sign, Carrot Top hollered like a banshee. I heard a loud thudding splat. Another splat followed on the heels of the first.

Crouched in the weeds behind the tree, I couldn't see the Beetle, but I could hear hoodlums swearing and girls screaming. And then: "There he is . . . get him."

Carrot Top hit the ground behind me—jumped right out of that tree and ran off down the creek bed lickety-split. Nary a word to me.

A car door slammed. One hoodlum followed Carrot Top and the other came after me. Scared witless, I bolted from the weeds and sprinted up the hill through the woods.

The hoodlum chasing after me tripped in one of our cardboard-lidded holes, fell headfirst into the deadfall, and twisted his ankle something awful. He hollered like a stuck pig, yelling that he'd broken his leg and thrashing around on the ground. I jumped another booby trap and ran on toward the Cave. Possum, Junior, and Lexi were well above it headed for the top of the hill.

As I clawed my way through the brush, my hoodlum made a

surprisingly quick recovery and staggered after me, dragging his bad leg and holding his head with both hands. I ran on between two sapling traps and cut diagonally across Sycamore Hill toward No-Man's-Land.

The hoodlum limped right into one of the sapling traps, which worked as advertised, knocking my hoodlum onto his back. But it didn't stop him. Stoked on adrenaline, he struggled to his feet again and labored on.

It was the sapling trap in No-Man's-Land that took the fight out of him. He lay flat on his face in pee germs for a long time, time enough for me to climb way above the Cave, nearer to the top of the hill. He got up and brushed the pee-soaked dirt out of his hair. He yelled, but I couldn't make out what he said. And then he turned and limped back toward the Beetle.

One of the blondes crunched the Beetle's gears into reverse and backed uphill to pick him up. Green ooze plastered the white leather seats, and the passenger blonde sat mopping slime off her face with a wad of Kleenex. The Beetle's rear bumper was decorated with a lime-green splat that dripped into the road.

By the time I topped the hill and found Lexi, Possum, and Junior, I couldn't breathe. I flopped onto the ground, lay on my back, and fought for air. Lexi wanted to know where Carrot Top was, but all I could do was shake my head. I had no idea. Last I'd seen of him, he was hightailing it down the creek with his hoodlum hot on his tail.

About that time, Junior pointed down the hill as Carrot Top's hoodlum walked along the Big Road back toward the intersection. He was drenched.

The four of us watched as he climbed into the Beetle and pointed uphill in our direction. We skedaddled on over the hill and circled around to the Bradley Smiths', where we hid in the basement until dark.

■　　■　　■

That was our last day on Sycamore Hill. We abandoned the hill, the Cave, Pee Rock, and the Deep Part, figuring the hoodlums knew our hideout and would likely torture us before chopping us into small pieces and feeding us to Big 'Un if they ever caught us.

After hearing what he'd missed, Chat snuck back to the Cave to find out whether the hoodlums had ransacked it like Carrot Top said they would. They hadn't, but Chat retrieved our cigar box to save it from plundering. Just in case.

40

Boobs

*Possum and Junior may have glimpsed their babysitter's boobs, and
Mrs. Littlejohn may have sunbathed mostly topless, but I hadn't
thought much about boobs until . . .*

One day when I was eleven and Carrot Top was twelve, Carrot
Top started talking about boobs. If one of us boys was likely to get
seriously interested in boobs a little ahead of schedule, it was Carrot
Top. He was a precocious kid, especially when it came to sinning.
Heck, by that age, Carrot Top had tasted his dad's bourbon straight
from the bottle and smoked three of his mom's cigarettes. If it
was sinful or unlawful, Carrot Top couldn't wait to get his hands
on it.

Well, I'd never paid much attention to boobs. I'd seen Mrs. Littlejohn sunbathing in her backyard. She had D-cup boobs, wore clothes

(including bikinis) that emphasized them, and didn't seem to mind folks looking at them as long as they were admiring and not leching. Possum and Junior talked about their babysitter's boobs from time to time. But it was Carrot Top's mentioning boobs that sparked my interest in learning more. We were boys without sisters, and therefore boys without access to in-house boobs, except of course mom boobs that, for some reason, weren't all that interesting. So Carrot Top and I went to Lexi's house. She was trying out a new slingshot on some lima-bean cans lined up along the stone wall that ran down their driveway.

She was the girl we knew best. She'd talk about anything. So we asked Lexi what she knew about boobs. Turns out, she had given them a lot of thought. She'd obviously grown curious about them long before we boys had and had quizzed her mom about them.

Mrs. Mallory had told Lexi all about boobs—when Lexi would probably get hers, about training bras needed to cover up budding nipples but not much else, about real bras and the various types and styles, about babies and milk in boobs, and on and on. Lexi said she'd show us her boobs when she got them, but she wasn't planning on getting them until she was thirteen or fourteen years old, which meant at least a two-year wait.

A few days later, Lexi said she'd told her mom about our discussion and her mom had whipped herself into such a froth over it, she'd pulled out some hair. Mrs. Mallory told Lexi she wasn't to talk to boys about boobs and there wouldn't be any showing them when she got hers. Girls did not go around showing their boobs, she said.

That was a setback.

So, we went to see Flo. She and Honey Bee were changing a baby-doll diaper. It was a messy one, according to Honey Bee.

Carrot Top asked Flo straight up if we could see her boobs when she got them. She said she'd show them to us but we'd have to play

House or School with her. And we'd have to play House or School first. She wasn't having us peek and run.

Unsolicited, Honey Bee said she wasn't showing her boobs to anybody but her husband and not until he had gotten her a house and a French poodle and a baby of her own. Honey Bee was no pushover.

41

Seek and Ye Shall Find

Comes an age when surprising things start to happen. I'll never forget the summer of '63 . . .

On summer nights, we McLeod boys finished our strawberry pie, asked to be excused, bolted from the supper table, and escaped into the great outdoor. Fireflies danced among the trees, frogs commenced their croaking along the creek, and kids poured into our backyard from every corner of the Hollow. Even Wiener. The only kid missing was Bobby, who, according to Mrs. Whitley, was too fragile for games played in the pitch-black dark where goodness-knows-what might trip her baby up and cause him harm.

For whatever reason, our yard was game central. We played kick-the-can, or capture-the-flag, or bear, or hide-and-seek. We mostly played kick-the-can, but I favored hide-and-seek because I won every time.

Hide-and-seek was therefore a tough sell. I had to promise to lose to get folks to play. Then I hid by myself in the dark in a cramped, smelly place for a really long time. And then I won. And gloated. And made the other kids hopping mad. The next night, I'd have to promise to lose again. And so on and so forth.

Not until the summer of my twelfth year did another kid stumble onto my secret.

"Eeeeeeck," Lexi squeaked.

The crickets around me went quiet.

"Shhh," I whispered.

"Sam, is that you? How'd you—"

"Shhh, Lexi. Get in here before they see you. Get your head down."

"There isn't—"

"C'mon, Lexi. Get in here before the whole neighborhood hears you."

Lexi crawled through the sticker bushes at the side of the Bird-songs' porch, collecting a few scratches along the way. Then through the hole in the latticework that hid the area under the porch from view and into the tiny crawl space that serviced a fat, leaky sewer pipe.

"It's too crowded in here," Lexi complained.

"Well, go find yourself another spot," I whispered. "And keep your voice down."

Technically, Lexi was right. It was too crowded in there. The crawl space was just large enough for a burly guy in coveralls to get his big wrench on the sewer pipe—not really big enough for a twelve-year-old kid. Certainly not big enough for two of them.

"Don't shush me," Lexi barked under her breath. "I'm not mak-ing—"

"Okay, okay," I pleaded in a barely audible voice. "Just please be a little quieter. And don't you dare tell anybody about this place."

"Oh, brother," Lexi muttered.

Summer nights in the Hollow were hot and sticky. We boys played in beltless mud-stained khaki shorts. Barefooted and bare-chested. Lexi and Flo traveled light, too. Just shorts and T-shirts. Only Honey Bee dressed for night games—a freshly pressed sleeveless blouse, co-ordinating shorts, colorful barrettes, and tennis shoes still warm from tumbling in the dryer. When we played hide-and-seek, Honey Bee rarely left her well-lit back porch and often yelled into the darkness, "Here I am. Here I am." Hoping for a little company.

Lexi shifted restlessly on the hard-packed clay beneath us. It was cool and smelled like a musty basement. Finally, she settled down, pressing her back against my chest, tucking her head under my chin and resting it on my extended left arm.

"Do you use deodorant yet?" she inquired.

"No, I don't need it," I said.

"Well, I think you do . . ." Lexi started.

"Shhh," I whispered.

Soon, the crickets under the porch resumed their courtship. Tree frogs tuned up in the darkness. The sewer pipe at my back dripped. And Lexi's breath settled into a soft rhythm.

Her hair tickled my nose. It smelled like the Mallorys' house—the distinctive smell of all Mallorys—something akin to homemade din-ner rolls just out of the oven. I tried to hold the smell in my nose only to have that heavenly scent interrupted by the sharp smell of Clorox from Lexi's T-shirt whenever she moved.

"Did you poot?" Lexi asked in an accusing voice.

"No. Maybe you did."

"I did not," Lexi said too loudly in her haughty voice. "It smells like a sewer under here."

"Well, there's a good reason for that—" I stopped abruptly.

We heard something moving not too far away—bare feet picking their way through the moist grass and then rustling in the bushes be-yond the latticework.

"I hear somebody in there," a voice boomed. It was Chat. "Don't make me come in there," he bellowed.

Instinctively, I reached around Lexi's belly and pulled her close—pulled her back from the latticework door perched precariously in its cutout space. Her stomach tensed and held while Chat poked a stick through the sticker bushes every few feet along the length of the Birdsongs' porch.

"You better come out of there," Chat warned, whacking the porch railing with his stick.

We lay perfectly still, not even breathing.

And then as quickly as he'd come, Chat wandered off, dragging his stick in the grass behind him, all bluster and bluff.

Lexi's stomach relaxed. Her T-shirt was warm and soft. Her stomach was soft, too. She felt good, but something about touching her there didn't seem right, so I started to pull my hand away. But she stopped me, put her hand over mine, and held it in place. On her stomach.

I felt the easy rise and fall of her breathing again. Occasionally something beneath my hand twitched or gurgled. And there we lay in that cool, musty place until Mrs. Littlejohn rang the bell at her back door summoning Flo home—signaling the end of our game.

So it wouldn't look like we'd been hiding together, Lexi returned to my house through the Littlejohns' backyard while I ran across the front yards and reappeared from the corner of the Whitleys' house. There I could see Bobby through the blinds in his room, sitting on his bed in his white cotton pajamas with the red-monogrammed shirt pocket, playing with a regiment of toy British soldiers.

When I saw Lexi the next day, she was halfway up the oak tree in the Whitleys' backyard, barefooted, wearing her dirty shorts and T-shirt from the night before. Her canteen—the one painted light blue with daisies on it—was strapped around her neck.

She was headed to the top of the tree, where she sat on hot summer days, a warm breeze rocking her while she watched the Hollow. Lexi often talked about sitting way up in that tree, surveying the Hollow, trying to remember every piece of it so she'd have it in her head when she went to bed, so she could see it in her mind before she fell asleep.

"What are you doing up there?" I asked, but already knew the answer.

"Sitting," Lexi said, not looking down.

A crow tried to land on a branch above Lexi's head, but moved on when she waved a hand at it.

"You coming up?" she asked.

"Nope," I said. "Going swimming with Chat."

"You playing tonight?" she asked.

"I reckon so," I said.

"If we play hide-and-seek, you mind if I hide with you?" she asked, looking down at me this time.

"That'd be fine," I said.

"Good," she said.

42

Sew It Up

This, too, shall pass . . .

As the summer of '63 came to a close, change was upon us.

We kids didn't have much experience with change. Oh, we got a little taller every year. And a year older.

Lexi and I were headed into seventh grade—moving over to the high school. That was change, but not unexpected.

Mrs. Littlejohn spent the first part of the summer as a brunette but switched back to blonde after the black coloring sweated onto, and ruined, her brand-new bikini top. That was change, but not unusual.

The neighborhood got a new milkman in August. That was change, but it didn't throw us off our stride too much.

Right on schedule, the girls started getting their boobs—just puffy nipples under their T-shirts, but enough to keep my interest up, ever hopeful they'd show them when they bloomed. Not much of a change, but welcome.

And then, real change: on Labor Day 1963, at the neighborhood social, at the tail end of that uneventful summer, the Witherspoons announced they were moving to Chicago.

The social came to a full stop. Even Possum stopped eating while Mrs. Witherspoon explained Mr. Witherspoon's new job, where they'd be living, and where Chat would go to school. Coco wept. So did the other moms. We kids stood silently around Chat. We had a lot of questions but had arrived at the age where asking questions wasn't cool. So we mostly tried to act like nothing was happening and wondered where Chicago was and whether we'd ever see Chat again.

It was the worst social ever. On that sad day, the fabric of our neighborhood frayed just a bit.

And then, in November, it was the Bradley Smiths' turn. Mr. Bradley Smith was promoted, Possum said. Whatever that meant. They were moving to Birmingham, Alabama, right after school let out for Christmas. Junior said they'd be back. They wouldn't be far from Nashville, he said. But they never came back.

The already-frayed fabric of the neighborhood got a run in it. It looked pretty bad.

After Junior and Chat moved away, Carrot Top went strange on us and hung out with a fast crowd of ne'er-do-wells. He called them the "cool kids." Lexi and I were in the same school building, but we weren't in the same classes and rarely saw each other.

A year later, I moved to a small, private boys' school. "Where you'll get more attention," Dad said, "and not be so distracted."

To make matters worse, Flo got her boobs in a big way but had second thoughts about showing them. She didn't care that I was willing to play House or School. And I thought a promise was a promise.

At that point, the fabric of our neighborhood tore. There was no hope of sewing it up. My childhood dissolved without any warning and the Crockett Rangers of Nashville, Tennessee, were no more.

43

On the Road
Jackson, Tennessee

When I was a kid, Uncle Pete's farm was better that Disneyland—big as the world and fat with adventures.

Today, the cornfield in front of the farmhouse is smaller than I remember it. Everything's smaller—the farmhouse, the old red barn, Uncle Pete's antique tractor, the falling-down chicken coop, Aunt Irma's kitchen garden, the fenced pasture behind the house.

The cats are gone, along with the chickens and pigs. The yard's quiet and still. Black Angus cows graze the hillside above the weed-choked pond. Grandy Jolley's 1964 yellow Caprice with the wide white sidewall tires is covered with a tarp, resting under a makeshift aluminum shed behind the barn. Like my Granddaddy McLeod, Grandy liked driving a fine car. "Couldn't bring ourselves to sell the thing," Aunt Irma says. "You know how Grandy loved it. Still runs like a top."

Mamie died years ago. Now her old room is full of worn-out furniture, faded photos in dusty frames, and unlabeled boxes full of who-knows-what.

"When did Mamie pass?" I ask.

"'Eighty-four," Uncle Pete says.

"Nineteen eighty-five," Aunt Irma corrects him.

"Close enough," Uncle Pete says.

"Didn't half know what to do with ourselves after she left us," Aunt Irma adds. "She was a blessing when you boys were around."

"She was a blessing all the time," Uncle Pete corrects her.

"We're even," Aunt Irma says.

Uncle Pete smiles.

The farmhouse was restored back in the nineties, but not changed much. The "never-ending erection" (as Aunt Irma calls it) spanned several years.

Out on the porch, my rocking chair squeaks to the beat of the fan turning leisurely above my head. The porch's bead-board ceiling is glossy blue, still discouraging wasps. A slight warm breeze stirs the pot-bound fern at the top of the steps. A faded green plastic tub lies next to the fern, waiting on Aunt Irma to collect the lettuce and parsley that's coming up in her garden. On the porch railing, there's a clear-glass saltshaker fitted with a rusty metal cap. It's nearly empty.

Bubba, a gangly puppy coonhound, is tugging at my pant leg trying to pull me out of my chair so I'll throw his slobber-covered tennis ball again, but I've settled in, a mug of hot black coffee here on the table beside me, and I don't plan to do a thing except sit for a while. Soak the place in.

Aunt Irma is nearly ninety years old. Uncle Pete's eighty-nine. Irma gets around with the aid of a cane Uncle Pete carved from a hickory branch. She moves slowly but steadily from the kitchen, where a pot of peeled potatoes simmers on the stove, to the porch to retrieve her vegetable-gathering tub, to the garden to pick whatever's ready, back to the kitchen, out to the porch again to check on me, around the side of the house to see whether Uncle Pete's headed our way for lunch, and back into the kitchen to set the table. The boundaries of her domain are well trodden.

I make like I'm getting up to help her, but only get halfway out of my rocker before she waves me down. "Don't need any help," she warns. "I know how to do this."

Uncle Pete wanders up from the barn and takes the rocker next to me, wiping his grimy hands on a grimier red rag.

"Tractor's on its last legs," he says, tossing Bubba's ball into the yard.

That's what he said fifty years ago.

"Think we should go in for lunch?" I ask.

"Nope," says Uncle Pete. "Irma don't like folks—particularly men-folks—in her kitchen till she calls 'em. Life's better-tolerable if we stay put."

"Fine by me," I say. "I'm developing a talent for sitting on this porch."

"Yep," says Uncle Pete. "Noticed that."

"What are we having for lunch?"

"Boiled potatoes," Aunt Irma says, coming out onto the porch, "smothered with white sauce, fried rabbit, spring peas, homemade applesauce, biscuits, those watermelon pickles you like, and pineapple upside-down cake from Mrs. Bell up the road. So, come on now, before your dinner gets cold."

"Wish you came for dinner more often," Uncle Pete says, prying himself from his rocker.

44

The Social

What goes around comes around . . .

Ripples of heat hovered over open fields of newly sprouted corn as I nosed my way down back roads to the Hollow. Nashville having spilled over old boundaries, I lost myself twice before finding my way to Hundred Highway and back into town.

Despite the detours, I was an hour early for the social, so I parked on Sycamore Hill Bridge, behind a sage-green Subaru with North Carolina tags, got out of my car, hiked up my britches, and looked up-hill, thinking I'd walk up to the Cave. Moccasin Creek babbled along underfoot. The air was fresh and cool in the shade of overhanging trees—a nice day for a short hike.

"It's still there," a woman's voice said.

Lexi, I thought, before turning around.

Her hair was silvery gray, lightly streaked with memories of gold, pulled into a clip on the back of her head. Crow's-feet marked the corners of still-youthful blue eyes. Her skin was weathered and tanned in the way of women who spend idle hours in the garden. A sleeveless flowery pink blouse hung untucked at her slender waist, above faded jeans. Her bare feet were strapped into all-terrain sandals. She'd gotten her boobs in a pleasant sort of way.

"Lexi, my goodness, you look just like yourself," I lied.

She laughed. "You're a smooth one, Sam McLeod. And just so you know, you don't look a thing like yourself."

She ran to me, reached around my ample middle, locked her hands into the small of my back, and rested her head on my chest.

"Nearly fifty years, Sam. Where in the world have you been? And that beard. I never pictured a beard."

"You like it?" I asked.

"Don't know yet," she replied honestly, releasing me but staying close. "Want to walk?"

"Sure," I said, not quite knowing what else to say.

"Mom sent me for paper plates," Lexi explained. "Stopped here on the way back. Walked along the creek a ways. Thought I'd hike up to the Cave."

"You read my mind," I said.

"Reading your mind was never much of a challenge." She smiled.

Lexi took my hand and pulled me up the road. We picked through the brambles and found our way to the Cave—not gone, but lost in the undergrowth and obviously forgotten. Except for a chipmunk rustling through the dense bed of leaves and twigs that covered the forest floor, the woods were eerily quiet. I cleared the brush at the Cave's entrance, squatted (without ripping my jeans), and stuck my head inside. It was empty—no forgotten treasures. A cool, but pungent breeze wafted up from the darkness beyond the ledge. The smells were familiar and comforting.

"See anything?" Lexi asked.

"Not much. Hard to believe we squeezed in here."

"You were smaller back then, Sam."

"Don't start, Lexi."

"Ooh, a bit sensitive are we? Can I take a look in there?"

"Sure."

While Lexi took a turn looking into the Cave, I looked out over the Hollow. A few of the houses had been painted different colors over the years. The Whitleys' old house was no longer pink. That was an improvement. Our redbrick house had been painted light beige. A two-door storage shed stood in the backyard where a crab apple tree had been. A new red-and-green-striped awning shaded the Birdsongs' porch. The Mallorys' tree house, painted dark brown (no longer Day-Glo orange), blended into the aging oak that supported it. A white delivery van moved silently along the Big Road. Otherwise, the Hollow looked much like I remembered it.

Lexi pointed to her backyard, where we could see a long table covered in a forest-green tablecloth, an assortment of low-slung beach chairs, and several people moving around them.

"My mom and dad," she said, "and your mom, I think. Took Mother forever to find your mom's new address and she never found her phone number. It was Mrs. Littlejohn who said she'd heard you were in Walla Walla. I didn't know it was a real place till I put the invitation in the mail. It's a miracle the thing got to you."

Lexi waded downhill through stiff briars and stood at the base of the old sycamore tree above Pee Rock, gazing up into its branches, absentmindedly tearing away a bit of its papery bark. Several branches were dead or dying, but most were thriving, covered in baby yellow-green leaves. She found a stick and scraped the accumulated deadfall of fifty years from the surface of Pee Rock and there she stood, stock-still, gazing downhill, playing back the memories in her head.

"I can't believe we did that," she mused.

"I can," I said.

We found our way back to the cars, over the bridge where Diesel and I spent part of a stormy night, and wandered up the Big Road. For most of an hour; we walked and talked, the unhurried talk of old friends. Lexi, without thinking, held on to my shirtsleeve, or a belt loop, or a finger.

She told of college life in Oxford, Mississippi, love at first sight, a fellow named Thurston, a rocky marriage to start, brief separation, the loss of a daughter to cancer, reconciliation, their two boys, Sam and Bo, moving to Chapel Hill, North Carolina, a house much like the Birdsongs' with a big front porch, the boys married now, off on their own, Thurston's teaching at the university, biking to work, Lexi's new landscaping business, her brothers—Zeke, a structural engineer in Minnesota, and Bo, still a little weird, but somehow surviving as a jazz musician in Santa Monica.

I rattled on about the University of Virginia, the spring of '70, the Grateful Dead, Annie, love, marriage, law school at Washington and Lee University, three daughters—Summer, Jolie, and Marshall, Chicago, Bethesda, Richmond, and then Seattle, law practice, business, Walla Walla and Detour Farm, Annie's alpacas and Rocky Mountain horses, the dogs and a cat that thinks she's a dog, weeds, the river's near flood, mountain views, and uncountable stars on moonless nights.

The sun glowed warm. A breeze fragrant with the smell of mowed lawns came and went. New leaves filled the trees. Willowy forsythia branches bowed under the weight of delicate yellow flowers. Robins hopped, stopped abruptly, listened, pecked among the dandelions, and tugged at earthworms found and stretched and snatched, after a brief tug-of-war, from the dirt. Our separate stories told, the years filled in, we strolled, well beyond the edge of the world as we'd known it.

■   ■   ■

Back in our cars, we drove up Old Orchard Lane, pulled into the Mallorys' graveled driveway, and wound our way around the side of their split-level house. We parked at the stone wall where Lexi had once pinged cans full of lima beans with bits of gravel slung from her slingshot and walked down familiar stone steps past the tree house toward neatly dressed picnic tables, pulled together end to end, set in the shade of the old oak, and covered in foil-wrapped platters, plastic-wrapped bowls, and glass vases full of daffodils. Several gray-metal folding chairs and a few beach chairs were scattered about.

Mrs. Mallory, twirling her hands in the air, hollered at us, "Well, it's about damn time."

Coco moved her walker in our direction, gave us each a one-armed awkward hug over her handlebars, and peppered us with questions about our trips "home." When did Lexi get to town? Was Thurston coming? What had I heard from our girls? Annie's new Rocky filly, had she arrived yet? And Lexi's boys, how were they doing? How was my visit to Jackson? What about Wiese? Did we go out? Where? And so on and so forth.

Mrs. Mallory, balding under wisps of white hair, stumbled into our midst, nearly toppling Coco and completely interrupting her train of thought. She looked frantic.

"You seen Bo?"

"Mom," Lexi interrupted. "Can't you say hello?"

"Oh my, Sam. Never pictured you with a beard. Your mom and I have had a nice visit. She's helping me set up. What a dear." Worry reappeared in her eyes. "I'm worried sick over Bo. He's supposed to be here." She looked me up and down again and said "Walla Walla" like it was a question (not a place). Then she shook her head, and turned on Lexi, grabbing the paper plates and begging her to call Bo.

Lexi rolled her eyes, dialed Bo's number on her cell phone, and pressed the phone to her mother's ear so she could hear Bo not answering.

"Classic Bo," Lexi said. "He'll show, Mom. He always does. You've got to relax. You're going to drive folks crazy with all that worry."

Mrs. Mallory shook her head and tugged at a strand of hair.

By twelve-thirty a crowd had gathered.

Mrs. Littlejohn's strapless dress matched the tablecloths she'd dropped off earlier in the morning along with the flowers. Her hair was as yellow as the daffodils and neatly poofed. She'd offered to bring dessert but Mrs. Mallory thoughtfully suggested table decorations instead. (If you'll remember, Mrs. Littlejohn couldn't even make a decent meatloaf.)

Flo, gray-haired and unadorned, stood beside her mother in a threadbare flannel shirt and carpenter-style jeans, looking over the top of her half-glasses, chatting with Mr. Mallory and my brother Mike about her furniture-making business in Virginia.

Mike had showed up wearing his green hospital scrubs and clogs. He'd spent a long night working in the emergency room—dealing with assorted stabbings, drug overdoses, and motorcycle accidents. He looked tired but said nothing was keeping him from a social.

Bobby Whitley, a purveyor of high-thread-count bed linens, sat at a table with Coco, looking very Brooks Brothers in his tortoiseshell glasses, navy blazer, stiff-collared baby-blue shirt with monogrammed cuffs, gabardine pants, and tasseled loafers. He brushed at unseen lint on his coat sleeve while Coco quizzed him about his mother's failing heart and Carrot Top's on-again, off-again problems with cocaine. "He's back in the tank," Bobby said. Coco nodded empathetically, like she understood what a tank was.

Mrs. Turner Smith unveiled her deviled eggs, eyeing the other platters on the table, while her boy Court (formerly Wiener), a lanky guy well over six feet tall, helped himself to a fudge brownie from a plate piled high with them.

"Flo brought 'em," he said. "Real good."

I cursed his bony frame as he held a half-eaten brownie between his teeth, wrapped another in a napkin, and slipped it into his shirt pocket.

"Watching my weight," I said.

"Good idea," said Wiener.

Lexi placed her mother's signature dish in the center of the table. "Where it goes," she mused. Abundant maraschino cherries floated in the translucent gold of jellied ginger ale.

The weathered picnic tables strained under the weight of Coco's tangy marinated vegetables, pimento cheese sandwiches, and fried chicken (enough to feed twice our number), Mrs. Witherspoon's fruit salad (fresh, except for the mandarin orange slices that came from a can) and ham biscuits (regular boiled ham, not the country ham everybody was hoping for), Mrs. Bradley Smith's green-tomato pies (just two, should have made three), a pickle tray, a quart jar of corn relish, Flo's brownies, several batches of chocolate-chip cookies, two picture-perfect cherry pies courtesy of Coco's hairdresser, Barbara, and a bright orange cooler full of fresh-squeezed lemonade made by Lexi.

The ladies hovered over the tables surveying their work, rearranging things that didn't need rearranging, wondering what was missing. Mrs. Mallory suddenly flung her hands into the air and stalked off toward the house, mumbling she'd forgotten to get her deviled eggs out of the refrigerator. Mrs. Turner Smith looked like she'd seen a ghost.

Name cards with pencil-thin green borders directed the seating. There was a place set for Mr. Birdsong at the head of the table. His fold-up metal chair sat empty. Mrs. Mallory rapped her fork on the side of Coco's chicken platter signaling a forthcoming speech, while Coco lifted herself off her bench seat, cleared her throat, and explained that a place had been set for Mr. Birdsong to represent those who were no longer with us. She recited the names: my dad, Mr. and Mrs. Birdsong, Mr. Bradley Smith, Mr. Turner Smith, Mr. Littlejohn, and Perry "Possum" Bradley Smith, who'd died much too young in the Vietnam War. The empty chair was a nice touch and a sad reminder that we males are a fragile bunch.

As if they'd rehearsed, Mr. Mallory stood as Coco lowered herself back onto the bench. He asked that we bow our heads and offered thanks for familiar foods, the gathering of old friends and family, the comfort of special places, a beautiful spring day, and good memories. We all said "amen" just like we'd always done and piled our plates high with the foods-of-socials-past. Foods full of meaning beyond good taste.

The sun moved imperceptibly overhead as we ate, talked, walked among the oaks to stretch our legs, debated the accuracy of memory, and laughed. Mrs. Littlejohn tugged constantly at the top of her dress. Mrs. Turner Smith wandered around carrying her tray of deviled eggs, asking if anybody wanted another one, while Mrs. Mallory's eggs disappeared. Lexi called Bo again. No answer. Wiener—I mean Court—ate brownies and asked Flo pointed questions about her love life. Flo played along, understanding what he really wanted—a renewed relationship built on FedEx deliveries of brownies. Bobby got a sprinkling of spring pollen on his jacket and asked Mr. Mallory if he had a coat brush. Mrs. Mallory went out to the front yard searching for Bo.

Mrs. Witherspoon caught us up on Chat and his life in Thailand—his Vietnamese wife, Lin, their both teaching English at a university there, and their three nearly grown daughters.

Mrs. Bradley Smith told about losing Mr. Bradley Smith to old age. "The old guy insisted on cremation," she said, a well-practiced look of disbelief on her face. "Wanted to be dumped in the backyard amongst the roses, but I spilled him on the patio before I got to the bushes. Urn broke into a thousand pieces. Ashes everywhere. I figure some of him made it to the garden, the way the wind was blowing." She hesitated, thought for a second, and then added, "Close enough, I guess."

I asked about Possum and Junior. She talked about Possum's dying in a helicopter crash in the Vietnam War and Junior's family living in Dallas, Texas—his precious wife, Karen, and a boy named Perry who'd just graduated from Duke and was going on to law school. She didn't know where.

Coco talked about moving to a duplex apartment after Dad died and the whereabouts of brothers Joey (Florida), Ricky (Brazil), and Harry (Franklin, Tennessee). Harry had planned to be at the social with his wife, Fran, and daughter, Holly, but the whole family was fighting a flooding basement, Mike said. Coco held on to hope that they'd put in an appearance before the day ended. I handled the "Why Walla Walla?" question.

Mr. Mallory told us about his prostate problem, including the details of his recent operation (you don't want to know), Zeke's bridge engineering work in Minnesota, and Bo's struggles to hang on to a job playing jazz trombone in Santa Monica, California.

Mrs. Littlejohn argued with Flo about the number of bedrooms in Honey Bee's Jacksonville, Florida, mansion. Was it seven or eight? Was Flo counting the nursery? Honey Bee had turned the nursery into a study. Hadn't Flo been there since Honey Bee redid everything? The nursery wasn't a nursery anymore, so you couldn't count the nursery as a bedroom.

They tended to agree on the white columns, two golden retrievers, the ten-foot hedge (maybe higher), two gardeners, four children—two boys, two girls—and a Daddy Warbucks named Robert, who owned his own defense contracting business. They also agreed on the number of bathrooms—nine.

Flo said under her breath, "Guess she showed her boobs."

By late afternoon, we'd lost Mrs. Turner Smith to a headache and another disappointing deviled egg performance. Mr. Mallory excused himself and went to take a short nap. (We never saw him again.) Flo and Wiener wandered off. Bobby and Mike played chess on one end of the picnic tables, using an acorn cap for a missing rook. Mrs. Mallory, still wringing her hands over Bo, busied herself with cleanup while Mrs. Littlejohn collected name cards and vases. That's when Coco stood again, showing as much enthusiasm as she could while clinging to her walker: "Stop. Oh my God! I almost forgot."

"Sam," she said. "Grab that box over by the tree and bring it here to Mr. Birdsong's chair."

"What?" I started.

"Just get it, Sam."

I retrieved the box, addressed to Coco from Annie. It wasn't heavy and didn't rattle.

Lexi handed me a knife. I slit the packing tape. Coco pulled at the box flaps and dumped handfuls of green plastic peanuts into an empty grocery bag.

"The Bowl," I said, pulling it from the box. Annie had retrieved it from my office, emptied the junk out of it, filled it with colorfully wrapped hard candies, and shipped it to Coco for the social.

"From Annie," I added.

I set it on the table.

We stared at it. Lexi touched it lightly and ran her index finger around the Bowl's well-worn edge. She fingered the candies. Picking up a piece and putting it back. Picking up another and putting it back. "I can't choose," she whispered, reciting her old line, before the tears welled up in her bright eyes and spilled over. Flo wept, too.

The sun disappeared as we said our good-byes, promising, as reunion-goers must, that we'd do it again *soon*.

I handed the Bowl to Flo.

"It's been gathering dust in my office for a long time," I said. "Maybe you'd like to hold it for a while, and then pass it on."

"Nice idea," she said. "I'll do that. Thanks, Sam. I'll never forget this."

Mrs. Witherspoon wrote Chat's address on a napkin and handed it to me, gave me a big hug, and begged me to write him.

"I will," I promised. "I will."

Coco left, asking when I'd be along.

"Soon," I said, "I'll be along after we finish cleaning up."

There wasn't much to do. Lexi rinsed out the empty cooler with a garden hose and toted it to the garage while I put the last bag of trash in the can at the corner of the house. When I turned to say my good-byes, Lexi was standing between my car and me.

"C'mon," she said.

"Where?"

"You'll see."

She grabbed my little finger in the half-moon light and pulled me back down the stone steps and across their backyard toward the Whitleys' old house.

"Lexi," I whispered. "What are you thinking? We can't go wandering into somebody else's yard in the middle of the night. We'll get shot. The Whitleys don't live here anymore, do they? We can't just—"

"Shhh," Lexi said.

At the old oak tree, she turned, looking out across the neighborhood yards toward the hills that marked the edge of the Hollow, playing those old movies in her head again. I leaned against the tree trunk, pressing my back against its ancient skin.

"Look," she whispered.

The air was crisp now, the humidity having fallen out of it. The night was unusually quiet, no crickets or frogs, just the rustling of a light but steady breeze and the faint burbling of the creek in the distance. The Hollow, bathed in soft moonlight, lay silent—its houses, trees, and the hills beyond visible only as moon shadows. A lonely light glowed from the Birdsongs' porch.

Lexi, still in her sleeveless shirt, shivered, moved in front of me, backed into my belly, laid her head back on my chest, and pulled my arms around her, my hands resting comfortably on her stomach, her hands resting on mine.

"Cold," she said, shivering, while she snapped mental pictures to add to those she'd taken years ago from this very spot and filed away.

Her stomach was warm. Her breathing was easy. Her hair tangled in my beard and I inhaled the smell of freshly baked dinner rolls—the smell of all Mallorys.

"Remember?" she asked.

"Yes," I said.

"Good," she said.

If I remember correctly (something I rarely do), the whole point of writing this book was to get in touch with my deep-fried roots and discover the meaning of life. Annie said if I did, the weight thing would take care of itself. She promised.

Well, what can I say?

PHOTO BY SQUARE PIXEL MEDIA

STILL BIG-BONED SAM

HEIGHT: 5 feet 10½ inches

WEIGHT: 230 pounds

CLOTHING SIZE: XL (sometimes, XXL)

After taking a gander at that photo, you're probably thinking my trip and self-reflection were a big waste of time. After all, no one ever knows for sure whether he's discovered the meaning of life. And I didn't shed fifty pounds or regain the lost inch of height. And I still haven't seen my high cheekbones, the outline of my ribs, or my penis without the aid of a mirror.

But I've been thinking since I took that trip, several months ago now, about what stood out: special places, foods full of memories, family, friends, the incredible women who devoted so much of themselves to my life, the great lessons, and the old stories. It was the trip of a lifetime.

My ample middle didn't seem to diminish anybody's affection for me. If anything, folks seemed to take some pleasure in the fact that I'm well fed. And come to think of it, their wrinkles, walkers, graying hair, and flabby upper arms didn't diminish my affection for them, either.

Like Charlie said, my weight's not messing with my health. At least it's not right now. So maybe it's not worth worrying over too much. Maybe big-boned is just the way I am. After all, I am a Jolley.

I told Annie what I was thinking. She smiled and nodded. "Not at all surprised," she said. "It happened just the way I said it would."

"*What?*" I said. "How could you possibly look at me and say—"

"Well, you discovered the meaning of life, didn't you? At least, I think you did—all those characters, the places that mean so much to you, sustenance steeped in history, and the incredible lessons. That's where you find meaning in your life, Sam. It's where you always have. Think about those long-winded stories you're always telling. They're all about those people, the places, the food, and the lessons.

"Miss Fleming was right, you know. Maybe it's time you exercised some of that creativity—it's there, it's just a little rusty. Why don't you write your stories down? Maybe make a book out of 'em."

"But—" I started.

"And the weight thing took care of itself like I said it would. Maybe not the way you expected, but the way it was supposed to. Your heft's not the important thing, Sam. It's part of who you are. You don't want to change that.

"Now go write those stories down before you forget them. I bet the worries will go plum away."

"But—" I tried to get a word in, but Annie was all wound up and closing in on fundamental truth. She's hard to slow down when she's closing in on truth.

"Lordy, Lordy, Lordy, Sam! Give it up with the buts. I know it's hard for you, honey—struggling through life without the emotional intelligence God gave a stinkbug—but move your thinking forward just one little notch. It's as plain as the nose on your face. It all worked out fine."

Well, I have thought about it now.

I have to admit Annie's got an interesting way of seeing things. Once again, she may be onto something.

And even if she's not, let's say she is.

Annie likes to have the last word on things.

COCO RULES

Figured I'd collect these in one place so you'll have them in case you decide you want to start living your life "the Coco way."

If you feel like hitting somebody, do it before you get in the car.

If you're going to eat a lot, you must look good doing it.

Don't aggravate the relatives and don't wipe your nose on your sleeve.

Always sit in the front pew below the pulpit.

If I'm cold, you'll wear your sweatshirt. End of discussion.

Whether you like it or not, you'll take a bite. It doesn't matter what *it* is. It doesn't matter what *it* looks like. It doesn't matter what *it* smells like. You are going to take a bite. And you are not going to hold your nose, or gag, or say anything bad about *it*.

Only one pickled shrimp before a party.

No sledding into the Big Road.

If you're going to jail, pack a suitcase.

No experimenting with chemicals in the presence of your brothers. When you blow yourself to Kingdom Come, you are not taking your brothers with you.

When running away, take more than one peanut-butter-and-jelly sandwich.

No messing with my Vidalias!